11 Holiday DIY Small Talks

FOR ACTIVITY DIRECTORS AND GROUPS

Daphne Simpkins

Quotidian Books

Montgomery, AL

Copyright © 2020 Daphne Simpkins

All rights reserved. No part of this publication may be reproduced, distributed or transmitted in any form or by any means, including photocopying, recording, or other electronic or mechanical methods, without the prior written permission of the publisher, except in the case of brief quotations embodied in critical reviews and certain other noncommercial uses permitted by copyright law. For permission requests, write to the publisher, addressed "Attention: Permissions Coordinator," at the address below.

Daphne Simpkins/Quotidian Books

Montgomery, Alabama

11 Holiday DIY Small Talks for Activity Directors and Groups/ Daphne Simpkins —1st ed.

ISBN 978-1-7320158-5-2

Contents

Seasons Greetings 6

#1 Charles Dickens' A Christmas Carol 9

#2 It's a Wonderful Life (Really!) 21

#3 What'll I Do? A Story about Irving Berlin 45

#4 Irving Berlin's Holiday Inn 55

#5 Irving Berlin's White Christmas 75

#6 Miracle on 34th Street 95

#7 I Love to Whistle! 107

#8 The Andy Griffith Christmas Show 113

#9 The Bethlehem Bible Story, Luke Chapter 2 127

#10 Tell Your Pandemic Story in the New Year 139

#11 Auld Acquaintances: A New Year's Talk 147

Sources & YouTube Addresses 155

Bonus Excerpt: Mildred Budge in Cloverdale 159

Books by Daphne Simpkins 175

About the author Daphne Simpkins 177

For my beautiful niece
Dr. Lola McCord

Every day is a good day.

—Mildred Budge

INTRODUCTION

Seasons Greetings

When classic movie director Frank Capra envisioned making movies, he said this was his goal: "My films must let every man, woman, and child know that God loves them, and that I love them, and that peace and salvation will become a reality only when they all learn to love each other."

Out of that vision, Capra made the Christmas classic "It's a Wonderful Life." It's the movie that Capra played each year for his own family during the Christmas holidays because he loved it. Capra said that after he died, he wanted people to say about him: "He's the man who made that movie 'It's a Wonderful Life.'"

This year as we are living through a pandemic and faced with a pretty cold winter, I wanted to tell people that message for Frank Capra. And to share with people some of what I know about Capra and the creation of that heartwarming movie and its important message: "God loves you and I love you and peace and salvation will only become a reality when we all learn to love each other." That's a hard message to deliver when we are all in a lockdown, keeping safe and, well, watching TV.

So, I figured I would write the Talk out and put some other Small Talks with it, and send it out in the world this winter for people who are trying to find a way to give Talks to groups but can't invite a speaker, like me. I would love to be with you, but I am in lockdown too. Even though I can't go, I hoped my Small Talks could. These Small Talks are written with the hope that they will be useful. The main ideas in each Talk are in bold type, to be read—and then to be paraphrased if you like. Or, you can just read the Small Talk as it is written. They are written to be read.

So, what follows are 11 Small Talks for the holidays—Christmas to New Year's.

The first six Talks are specifically about Christmas with a slight veering to a Small Talk about Irving Berlin because he wrote "White Christmas." That song changed the Christmas musical landscape!

The next five Small Talks that follow the #6 Talk, *Miracle on 34th Street,* are more general.

Each Small Talk has a Synopsis page to help you decide whether this is one that your group will like. There are some tips on how to prepare for the Talk and to give it. The Small Talk itself follows. Next, when appropriate, biographical sketches are included after the Small Talk in case your members want to know more about the people involved. That list of biographies is not comprehensive—just enough to flesh out the Small Talk. They are mostly anecdote based. When possible, there is a quick story of some kind to tell about the person. You can use how much of these brief biographies as you have time to include in your group's get-together. Each Small Talk stands on its own.

Here are the 11 Small Talks:

1. Charles Dickens' A Christmas Carol
2. It's a Wonderful Life (Really!)
3. What'll I do? A Story about Irving Berlin

4. Irving Berlin's Holiday Inn
5. Irving Berlin's White Christmas
6. Miracle on 34th Street
7. I Love to Whistle
8. The Andy Griffith Christmas Show
9. The Bethlehem Bible Story
10. Tell Your Pandemic Story in the New Year
11. Auld Acquaintances A New Year's Talk

If you're wondering why there's a Small Talk about whistling, it's because Bing Crosby, who starred in both *Holiday Inn* and *White Christmas*, is a whistler. He whistles spontaneously, kind of like how we may start to hum all of a sudden. That got me thinking and wondering about whistling in old movies. A lot of whistling happens—enough to create for you a #7 Small Talk about whistling that is more whimsical than educational.

I hope you can use and enjoy these Small Talks. They are written with the kind of love and vision that Frank Capra had about making movies. Each Small Talk celebrates the common man and woman—and they encourage people to believe that just being together wherever we are and thinking about something together is a way to learn to love each other better.

Go tell them!

SMALL TALK #1

#1 Charles Dickens' A Christmas Carol

Charles Dickens

Synopsis
Small Talk #1
Charles Dickens' *A Christmas Carol*

Type: Informative

One sentence summary: This Talk looks back at the original source for the authentic ideas behind Scrooge, Tiny Tim, and the benediction of "God bless us everyone."

Why I wrote this Small Talk: There have been so many versions of this story that we forget how good the original story is. I wanted to remind people.

Why Your Group Will Love This Talk: Dickens' original theme of keeping Christmas is about becoming more aware of others and taking responsibility for being kinder and more considerate—generous, too.

Tags: Charles Dickens, *A Christmas Carol,* Scrooge, Bob Cratchit, Tiny Tim, Lionel Barrymore

What you'll need: The air date if your group is watching the movie together or when they may choose to hear your remarks and then retire to their own room to watch it; or the DVD or Blu-Ray or a recorded version on your DVR; or the ability to play a movie on demand from a premium television service.

Good to Know: For Kindle users in your group, the novel *A Christmas Carol* by Charles Dickens is a FREE download from Amazon or it was October 2, 2020.

Talking Tip: To build audience involvement, you can print out the excerpts from the Talk and ask people in the audience to read the excerpts from Dickens' original story when you reach that part in the Talk. I will post the 4 excerpts used in this Talk on the Quotidian Books Facebook page if you prefer to find them there.

Audience Icebreaker: "Which expression is Scrooge most famous for?" The answer: "Bah! Humbug," of course. Humbug asserts that something is nonsense or gibberish. You can conclude this Talk if it suits you with the question: "Which expression is Tiny Tim most famous for?" The answer: "God bless us everyone." That question and answer create a great farewell (a benediction, really) for this Talk.

Small Talk #1
Charles Dickens' *A Christmas Carol*

Charles Dickens' *A Christmas Carol* has been reimagined in different books and movies over and over again since Dickens' original *Carol, a ghost story—really!--* was first published in 1843.

But the reality of why Dickens wrote *A Christmas Carol* and its spread of the Christmas message is unique to him, for Dickens gave us two primary characters that are now iconic: Scrooge and Tiny Tim.

Dickens had one major objective in mind when he created the story, but it was a very big goal: Charles Dickens wanted to change cold, cold hearts.

A Christmas Carol's Beginnings....

Charles Dickens had a problem in Victorian England. He couldn't sleep for worrying about it. Misery abounded around him. He saw children suffering from workplace abuse and starvation. Adults, too.

Dickens felt a great urgency to help the poor, but he also knew that the people in Victorian England had become numb to the sight and plight of hungry, often sick children, their living and working conditions, and the snowballing harmful effects of widespread poverty.

How do you warm a cold human heart?

Dickens instinctively understood the short-lived effect of a sympathetic appeal. A repeated cry for help and sympathy gets your attention at first, but over time the repeated sight or message of it wears people out. People become numb to the sights, sounds, and overwhelming burdens of profound human need. Dickens needed something to shake up his neighbors and fellow citizens—to stir them to help the poor by seeing the suffering of others as an opportunity to help rather than as a burden they can't afford to bear.

Dickens paced London streets at night looking for an answer!

Walking the streets of England at night, Dickens imagined a story that might move people out of the inertia of not caring. When he finally devised his plot, Dickens went home and wrote *A Christmas Carol*.

After Dickens writes Scrooge's story, the problem is clear: Ebenezer Scrooge does not have the spirit of Christmas in his heart.

Here are four excerpts from the original story by Dickens:

Set up for the first excerpt: Scrooge doesn't keep Christmas, and his nephew knows it.

When nephew Fred greets his Uncle Scrooge, he says hello with a prayer for his uncle's salvation tucked inside the greeting: "God save you!"

Excerpt 1 begins here:

"A merry Christmas, uncle! God save you!" cried a cheerful voice. It was the voice of Scrooge's nephew.

"Nephew! Returned the uncle, sternly. "Keep Christmas in your own way, and let me keep it in mine."

"Keep it!" repeated Scrooge's nephew. "But you don't keep it."

"Let me leave it alone, then," said Scrooge. "Much good may it do you! Much good it has ever done you!"

"There are many things from which I might have derived good, by which I have not profited, I dare say," returned the nephew. "Christmas among the rest. But I am sure I have always thought of Christmas time, when it has come round—apart from the veneration due to its sacred name and origin, if anything belonging to it can be apart from that—as a good time; a kind, forgiving, charitable, pleasant time; the only time I know of, in the long calendar of the year, when men and women seem by one consent to open their shut-up hearts freely, and to think of people below them as if they really were fellow-passengers to the grace, and not another race of creatures bound on other journeys. And therefore, uncle, though it has never put a scrap of gold or silver in my pocket, I believe that it has done me good, and will do me good; and I say, God bless it!"

Excerpt 2: Dickens describes Scrooge carefully. Scrooge is a cold man!

"Oh! But he was a tight-fisted hand at the grindstone. Scrooge! A squeezing, wrenching, grasping, scraping, clutching, covetous, old sinner! Hard and sharp as flint, from which no steel had ever struck out generous fire; secret, and self-contained, and solitary as an oyster. The cold within him froze his old features, nipped his pointed nose, shriveled his cheek, stiffened his gait; made his eyes red, his thin lips blue; and spoke out shrewdly in his grating voice. A frosty rime was on his head, and on his eyebrows, and his wiry chin. He carried his own low temperature always about with him; he iced his office in the dog-days, and didn't thaw it one degree at Christmas."

Excerpt 3: How others in Dickens' story responded to Scrooge:

"Nobody ever stopped him in the street to say, with gladsome looks, 'My dear Scrooge, how are you? When will you come to see me?' No beggars implored him to bestow a trifle, no children asked him what it was o'clock, no man or woman ever once in all his life inquired the way to such and such a place, of Scrooge.

Excerpt 4: Even a blind man's dog sees Scrooge for who he is and has an opinion.

Even the blind men's dogs appeared to know him; and when they saw him coming on, would tug their owners into doorways and up courts; and then would wag their tails as though they said, "no eye at all is better than an evil eye, dark master!"

No one feels this coldness in Scrooge more than his employee Bob Cratchit.

Cratchit's working conditions are merciless. Scrooge provides Cratchit one piece of coal to warm himself by and the light of one candle. Dickens says that Cratchit doesn't have enough imagination to get warm from either one. Cratchit works on. With a family to feed, Cratchit bears the burden of the cold and Scrooge's company. Because he is not paid well, his family also suffers. His son Tiny Tim is hungry and needs medical help, but Cratchit is too poor to help his own boy.

And Christmas is still coming, poor or not!

Christmas is coming, but Scrooge's cold heart is costing Bob and his family the joy of the season until one night—one fast-moving, eventful night—Scrooge's former business partner Jacob Marley, who has been dead as a doornail for seven years, pays his old business partner a visit with the alert to his old colleague (friend is too strong a word here) that three Spirits are coming to show Scrooge what he needs to know.

Why is Jacob Marley sent?

And while we're asking questions....

Why is the wretched spirit of Marley draped in chains?

Dickens says it better, but the gist of Marley's terrible dead-as-a-doornail condition is that he paid so little attention to others while alive that he must now drag the weight of his sins of omission around with him, forever unable to engage with others as he should have when he could have been of service to his fellow man.

Marley regrets the lost opportunities of his life. He warns Scrooge to pay attention to what the Ghosts who are coming will show him and choose more wisely than he did.

The story is riveting and should be re-read for pure pleasure.

The Ghosts bring three messages:

The **Ghost of Christmas Past** shows how a neglected little boy named Ebenezer Scrooge turned inward, ultimately, choosing a solitary, self-absorbed life. Ebenezer Scrooge at one point does fall in love and have a fiancé, but by this time, he has begun to find his satisfaction in business and making money. His fiancé releases him from their engagement, explaining to him that he has devoted himself to Gain—not to her and to love.

The **Ghost of Christmas Present** introduces Scrooge to people who are in the moment of celebrating others. He sees his nephew Fred truly keeping Christmas with love expressed out loud for others.

The **Ghost of Christmas Future** shows Scrooge what happens after he dies. Unless something good happens for the Cratchit family (unless Scrooge changes!), Tiny Tim will die of his ailment and the poverty that caused it. Scrooge sees in this vision of the future after his death that his own paltry possessions, for which he has basically given his life, are stolen and hocked. He sees someone who owes him money relieved he is dead. In short, what Scrooge experiences in this final vision is that his life is not valued by others because he was so self-absorbed and stingy. His possessions for which he traded his life have little value. His absence is not mourned. His death is a relief to others: people who know him and people who owe him money.

People can change. Scrooge proves it!

Miraculously, upon waking, Ebenezer Scrooge realizes he has the time and opportunity to act upon the change in his heart.

Scrooge resolves to do better immediately—to be generous, to be aware of how others are experiencing life, to be kinder to others. He helps Bob and Bob's crippled son, Tiny Tim, who like Scrooge becomes an icon of Dickens' *A Christmas Carol*.

Dickens intended message?

When we close off our hearts to the sights and sounds of Tiny Tim and all the children like him, we choose a Scrooge existence. And Christmas? It, too, becomes an icon that represents not only a time at the end of the year in the dead of winter—but becomes a way of being and thinking and living that is needed year-round. We just wake up to it, like Scrooge, in December, but we must practice the spirit of Christmas Present while it is today, whether it is the actual Christmas Day or not.

The ending of *A Christmas Carol* is a hopeful one, where not everyone gets better and immediately has enough to eat, but where the person who can help others takes responsibility for trying to improve the quality of life for others.

Old Man Scrooge changes, and that is the beginning of hope. A cold heart can warm up.

A Christmas Carol has been told in a number of ways. The event of being shown who you are has been adapted in a variety of retellings with main characters changing. None of the later versions are more potent than the story itself published by the determined Charles Dickens in December, 1843

Selected movie versions of Dickens' tale that may be familiar to you:

A Christmas Carol 1938 starring Reginald Owen
A Christmas Carol 1951 Alastair Sim --considered the most popular version of this story
Scrooge 1970 Albert Finney
Scrooged 1988 Bill Murray
A Flintstones Christmas Carol 1994

∼

The backdrop of Christmas as a setting for personal change occurs often in other favorite movies enjoyed between Thanksgiving and Christmas. But the goal of the storyteller is not so much about helping to promote social justice or alleviate suffering; it is more often about one person experiencing a coming-of-age moment--changing from one way of thinking to another way of being and all for the better.

Christmas messages abound in Christmas movies!

Another film that created an iconic set of characters is Frank Capra's *It's a Wonderful Life*. The Scrooge character in *It's a Wonderful Life* is played by the incomparable Lionel Barrymore. Mr. Barrymore was a natural choice for the movie role as he had been giving voice to Scrooge annually on the radio for the previous twenty years.

SMALL TALK #2

#2 It's a Wonderful Life (Really!)

Clarence the Angel and George Bailey in *It's a Wonderful Life*

Synopsis
Small Talk #2
It's a Wonderful Life, (Really!)

Type: Informative

Summary: Director Frank Capra's vision for this movie was to encourage every viewer—every ordinary person—that his or her life is highly significant.

Why I wrote this Small Talk: After I read Frank Capra's autobiography, I was so moved by his vision for movie making and this one in particular I wanted to share what I had learned with others.

Why your group will enjoy this Small Talk: There are so many familiar faces in this movie, and your group members will enjoy hearing more about them. The biography of Jimmy Stewart that follows the Small Talk may be of particular interest. He was a ladies' man, and that surprises people who see him differently.

Tags: *The Greatest Gift,* Frank Capra, Jimmy Stewart, Donna Reed, Gloria Grahame, Beulah Bondi, Lionel Barrymore, Bedford Falls, 'Every time a bell rings an angel gets his wings', *The Best Years of Our Lives*, Margaret Sullavan, Henry Fonda.

What you'll need: The air date if your group is watching this classic movie together or in their rooms after your Talk; the DVD or Blu-Ray; or the capability to play the movie on demand from a premium television service.

Additional Resources: The colorized version of *It's a Wonderful Life* is available to watch free on Amazon Prime as of this date: 10/2/21. *The Greatest Gift,* as a Kindle book, costs about $10 on Amazon.

When to give the Small Talk: The Small Talk #2 It's a Wonderful Life (Really!) is ideal for any date between Thanksgiving and Christmas. Other occasions to use the biography about **'Good Sam' Jimmy Stewart** by itself could fit before any of his many very popular movies, including the Westerns, the Hitchcock movies, or ones with his real-life love interest Margaret Sullavan, *The Mortal Storm* or *The Shop Around the Corner.*

∼

John Cassavetes said about the influence of Frank Capra's work: "Maybe there really wasn't an America. Maybe it was only Frank Capra."

Small Talk #2
It's a Wonderful Life (Really!)

There are many reasons people watch *It's a Wonderful Life* every year

You love the look and feel of homey Bedford Falls, a small snowy American town where the story takes place. It's inhabited by working class people who are trying to make a living, make a home, be in love.

Director Frank Capra had a big goal in mind for this movie

The director Frank Capra explained why he wanted to tell this story in his autobiography, *The Name Above the Title:* "My films must let every man, woman, and child know that God loves them, and that I love them, and that peace and salvation will become a reality only when they all learn to love each other."

That's the short and true reason Frank Capra loved the original story, which began as a self-published Christmas card by Philip Van Doren Stern, who sent his 24-page booklet to his friends and family in 1943. *(The Greatest Gift* was published the next year.) That original story that became *It's a Wonderful Life* was originally called *The Greatest Gift.*

Capra and Stewart were two men back from the war and looking for work

The Greatest Gift came to Capra and to the star of the movie, Jimmy Stewart, after WWII, when each man was wondering if he could pick up his career in the movie business after he returned from active military service.

You can imagine how they felt. Each man had found success in movie making, and then he went off to war.

Life and change and popularity happen quickly in Hollywood, and neither man knew whether there would be a place for him and the gifts he brought to the work of cinematic storytelling.

The war caused Capra to want to make a different kind of movie

Capra's vision of the kind of movie he wanted to make changed while he was away. He returned home wanting more originality and truth in his movie's stories—more individuality. For the first movie made by his new company, Capra wanted a story that would signal to others what kind of stories they could expect from his company, Liberty Films.

Capra explains how *The Greatest Gift* became *It's a Wonderful Life*

"I read the original idea—a few typewritten pages bound in Christmas covers. It was the story I had been looking for all my life! Small town. A man. A good man, ambitious. But so busy helping others, life seems to pass him by. Despondent. He wishes he'd never been born. He gets his wish. Through the eyes of a guardian angel he sees the world as it would have been had he not been born. Wow! What an idea. The kind of idea that when I got old and sick and scared and ready to die—they'd still say, 'He made *The Greatest Gift*.'"

Three screenwriters had already tried to convert *The Greatest Gift* into a movie script and failed before Capra took over

Capra explained: "Later I read the three scripts by Trumbo, Connelly, and Odetts. They were wide of each other and wider of the simple beauty of the original idea.

"I saved a few of Odets's opening scenes…….But the Hacketts (Albert Hackett and Frances Goodrich) were perceptive, human writers. I hired them to write a new script that stuck closer to Van Doren Stern's original concept. Then I worried about an actor to play the man."

"Of all actors' roles I believe the most difficult is the role of a Good Sam who doesn't know that he is a Good Sam."

Capra wanted Jimmy Stewart to play 'Good Sam' character George Bailey

"I knew one man who could play it. From an enlisted private he had worked his way up to a colonel leading a squadron of B-24 bombers. Jimmy Stewart. He had just been discharged. I spoke to Lew Wasserman, the MCA agent who handled Jimmy, told him I wanted to tell Jimmy the story. Wasserman said Stewart would gladly play the part without hearing the story. But I insisted."

"If Jimmy was as scared as I was about making another film, I'd like to know it...."

"A meeting was arranged in Sam Briskin's apartment. Lew brought in Jimmy. He was older, shyer, ill at ease. My butterflies fluttered. It was four years since I had last told a story to an actor. It was six years since Stewart had heard a story from a director. Jimmy listened quietly—bored, I thought. The story evaporated into thin air, flew out the window; like one of those fragile, gentle things that 'if you touch them, they vanish.'

Frustration hit me. I leaped to my feet. '...I haven't got a story......Forget it, Jimmy.'"

Time passed while each man wrestled with *The Greatest Gift's* concept and his part in the project.

Stewart said *yes*, and Capra's vision of the story returned

Capra recalls: "Two weeks later Stewart signed for the part. The story came back to me more beautiful than ever."

It's a Wonderful Life was not everyone's favorite movie that year

Originally, *It's a Wonderful Life* received mixed reviews from critics. And, it was eclipsed by another powerful movie that would win the Best Picture Oscar that year: *The Best Years of Our Lives* starring Fredric March and Myrna Loy.

Both men tried to figure out why their comeback movie didn't connect immediately with an audience.

In the biography by Michael Munn called *Jimmy Stewart: The Truth Behind the Legend*, Munn suggests that Stewart believed people were just more ready for a story/ movie at that time that would explore the effects of the war on families. *The Best Years of Our Lives* did that and dominated the awards and the box office.

Later, *It's a Wonderful Life* found its audience with television

But that humble beginning did not keep *It's a Wonderful Life* from finding an audience. Television did that for this movie, which explains how so many people have come to find the comfort and encouragement that Frank Capra had in mind when he explained who he envisioned as the people who needed to experience this story.

Capra described at length the people he wanted to see it

It's a Wonderful Life would be….

"A film to tell the weary, the disheartened, and the disillusioned; the wino, the junkie, the prostitute; those behind prison walls and those behind Iron Curtains, that no man is a failure!

"To show those born slow of foot or slow of mind, those oldest sisters condemned to spinsterhood, and those oldest sons condemned to unschooled toil, that each man's life touches so many other lives. And that if he isn't around it would leave an awful hole.

"A film that said to the downtrodden, the pushed-around, the pauper, 'Heads up, fella. No man is poor who has one friend. Three friends and you're filthy rich.'

"A film that expressed its love for the homeless and the loveless; for her whose cross is heavy and him whose touch is ashes; for the Magdalenes stoned by hypocrites and the afflicted Lazaruses with only dogs to lick their sores.

"I wanted it to shout to the abandoned grandfathers staring vacantly in nursing homes, to the always-interviewed but seldom-adopted half-breed orphans, to the paupers who refuse to die while medical vultures wait to snatch their hearts and livers, and to those who take cobalt treatments and whistle—I wanted to shout, "You are the salt of the earth. And *It's a Wonderful Life* is my memorial to you!"

The movie didn't win the hoped-for awards, but it did win the hearts of viewers over time

While the movie didn't win the awards that year that one might have expected, in 1998 the American Film Institute named it as one of the 100 top American films ever made. Its rank for all time? #11.

But *It's a Wonderful Life* is now quite often the first choice people make when they want to settle down with a good Christmas movie to launch the season each year.

Small Talking Points about the Players....

The Players

George Bailey played by Jimmy Stewart
Mary Hatch Bailey played by Donna Reed
Ma Bailey played by Beulah Bondi
Clarence the Angel played by Henry Travers
Violet Bick played by Gloria Grahame
Mr. Potter played by Lionel Barrymore
Fellow on the porch played by Dick Elliott

James Stewart (May 20, 1908-July 2, 1997)

Jimmy Stewart

Jimmy Stewart was born in Indiana, Pennsylvania on May 20, 1908, where his dad owned a hardware store.

Jimmy's given name was James Maitland Stewart, and in his earlier days before he became an actor, Jimmy wanted to be an architect. He could work with geometrical shapes pretty well, but Mr. Stewart's boy was a poor academic student. Jimmy's lack of scholarly ability did not prevent his dad, a shopkeeper, from sending him to Princeton, where Stewart scraped by academically, but surprisingly, had a way with the ladies—and an accordion.

The accordion was a useful instrument, which his dad had given to his son after a circus came to town. Jimmy's dad had extended credit to the circus performers, who ultimately couldn't pay their bill. They gave Mr. Stewart the accordion instead of settling the bill with cash. Mr. Stewart handed the accordion off to Jimmy and said, "Son, learn to play this."

Learning the accordion paid off for Jimmy

That portable musical instrument opened doors for Jimmy in his early days of looking for work in the theatre. Jimmy was pretty good at playing it, and the skill helped him earn roles on stage. An accordion, unlike a piano, is a portable keyboard that operates with bellows. Air moves across reeds inside to make sounds. It's lightweight and can be carried on and off a stage. And later when Stewart starred in Westerns, he used it as a prop as he did in the western *Night Passage (1957)*

Boy! Did women like Jimmy Stewart!

While Stewart was finding himself as an actor, he was also finding his way romantically. Women liked him. Boy, did women like Jimmy Stewart! Lots of women at every party liked tall, too-thin Jimmy Stewart. When fellow actor Henry Fonda accused Jimmy of stealing his girl, Stewart defended himself: "I didn't steal her. She stole me."

Many women tried to steal Stewart, but the one that got away was Henry Fonda's first wife Margaret Sullavan. Fonda and Sullavan were married in 1931 and divorced in 1933. When Stewart worked with Sullavan, he fell for her hard. It was mutual. By all accounts, Sullavan and Stewart loved each other all of their lives, but because of her history with his best friend Henry Fonda, Stewart did not pursue marriage with Sullavan. However, he did co-star in four movies with her. *The Shop Around the Corner* and *The Mortal Storm* are two of the most popular.

Later, Stewart dated many women and became serious for a while with all-American girl Dinah Shore, only to find out right before they were going to say "I do" that she had fallen in love with actor George Montgomery.

Stewart's heart wasn't broken for long. He dated Olivia de Havilland, Loretta Young, Norma Shearer, Marlene Dietrich, and many others. Stewart had romantic relationships with many ladies in cinema to the point that he earned the newspaper nickname the Great American Bachelor, not marrying until he was in his forties.

But Stewart finally found the right woman. In August of 1949, Jimmy married Gloria Hatrick McLean, who understood his widespread appeal to both women and audiences. She also recognized his temper. Munn recounts her words in his biography of Stewart. "Gloria said, 'Jimmy had a temper. A rage that he learned to control.'"

But some say that controlled rage is what fueled many of Stewart's finest performances, like the one he gives when he begins to lose control and consider suicide in *It's A Wonderful Life*.

But for the most part Jimmy Stewart is considered a genial, kind, amiable eccentric who befriends a six-foot imaginary rabbit in the movie *Harvey*, plays a shrewd lawyer in *Anatomy of a Murder*, and shows up as a good guy hero in Westerns and Alfred Hitchcock movies, including *Vertigo* and *Rear Window*.

Henry Fonda said of his long-time friend, "The role of George Bailey was most like Jimmy. When you see George, you see Jimmy's personality magnified."

Jimmy's marriage to Gloria was a long and happy one, ending only with her death from lung cancer in 1994.

Beloved Jimmy Stewart developed an irregular heartbeat after Gloria's passing. He died at home of a heart attack in 1997 at the age of 89. His last words to family nearby were: "I'm going to be with Gloria now."

Donna Reed (January 27, 1921-January 14, 1986)

Donna Reed as Mary Hatch

In *It's a Wonderful Life,* Donna Reed's character Mary falls in love with George Bailey when they are both school kids. Seated at a soda fountain where George is touting the glory of coconuts, the young girl leans forward to declare her love to him in his bad ear. Mary promises George Bailey: "I'll love you to the day I die."

All of us will, won't we?

In her vow, viewers know who Mary is, and we begin to understand how noble a soul George Bailey is to inspire such love and commitment in such a wholesome and faithful girl.

Their romantic relationship does not evolve smoothly. George is ambitious and wants to see the world away from Bedford Falls. Mary Hatch waits.

Life keeps happening in Bedford Falls and to the Bailey family.

In a moment of crisis, George's mother steers her son toward the good girl: "Mary is the kind of woman who can help you find the answers."

Reed's character in *It's a Wonderful Life* remains true to that description. And it is a role that fits much of what Donna Reed did on her television show *The Donna Reed Show* and other roles where she plays a steady-as-she-goes all-American housewife. The exception is when Reed was cast against type in *From Here to Eternity*, where she played a darker, sultry type of woman, a role for which she won the Academy Award for Best Supporting Actress in 1953.

At the height of television series *Dallas'* popularity, the producers asked Reed to replace Barbara Bel Geddes as the matriarch Miss Ellie for the Ewing clan. But Bel Geddes decided to return to her role after all, and Reed was dismissed with a million-dollar settlement for her trouble.

Donna Reed was married three times, the last time to Grover W. Asmus. She died of pancreatic cancer a few days before her 65th birthday.

Beulah Bondi (May 3 1889-January 11, 1981)

Beulah Bondi

It's a Wonderful Life was the fourth movie where Beulah Bondi called Jimmy Stewart, "Son." Other movies they co-starred in were *Of Human Hearts, Vivacious Lady,* and *Mr. Smith Goes to Washington.*

Like other film stars, Bondi migrated into television and appeared in a 1963 episode of Perry Mason: *The Case of the Nebulous Nephew.* Her final screen performance was in the popular family show *The Waltons,* for which she won an Emmy for her role in *The Pony Cart* (1976).

Bondi appeared in another Christmas classic, *Remember the Night,* starring with Barbara Stanwyck and Fred MacMurray. Yes, she played Fred MacMurray's mother too!   She played countless supporting roles and was successful during her long career.

 Bondi died of pulmonary complications after tripping over her cat at home. She was 91.

Henry Travers (Travers John Heagerty) Mar 5, 1874-Oct 18, 1965

Henry Travers

British-born Henry Travers became active in American theatre in 1917 and had a long and productive career playing characters mostly older than himself.

As the times changed, so did Henry Travers. He transitioned from the stage to movies, landing memorable roles in *Mrs. Miniver, Random Harvest, The Bells of St. Mary's,* and Alfred Hitchcock's *Shadow of a Doubt.*

Travers was married twice, the first time to Amy Forrest Rhodes from 1881-1954, when she passed away. He married again, this time in 1955 to Ann G. Murphy, who survived him.

He died at the age of 91 from natural causes.

Gloria Grahame (November 28, 1923—October 5, 1981)

Jimmy Stewart and Gloria Grahame

Town flirt Gloria Grahame turns heads in Bedford Falls when she walks down a street wearing a saucy dress that George Bailey admires. He pays her a compliment. Flipping her hair, she replies something like, "This old thing? I only wear this when I don't care how I look."

The Town Flirt sashays away, leaving behind gawkers and stopping traffic.

In real life and on the screen, Grahame was a head-turner. Her femme fatale appeal is part of her charm not only in this flirtatious girl role in *Wonderful Life,* but also in *Oklahoma,* where she played a girl who couldn't say no. She was featured also in the stylish movie *In a Lonely Place* with Humphrey Bogart. The movie was directed by Nicholas Ray, whom she later married.

Grahame starred in a series of popular movies, winning the Oscar for Best Supporting Actress for her performance in *The Bad and the Beautiful* (1952).

Not classically beautiful, Grahame had attitude and presence. Grahame became obsessed with her looks later in life and sought excessive plastic surgery for her face, which caused her many problems.

She had other concerns as well. Married unsuccessfully to three men, for her fourth marriage in 1960, Grahame married Anthony "Tony" Ray, her own stepson from her second marriage to Nicholas Ray and his first wife Jean. Grahame's fourth marriage caused quite a scandal, which hurt Grahame's career and personal and professional relationships with other people in Hollywood. They divorced in 1974.

Diagnosed with the return of cancer in 1980 that had been in remission since 1974, Grahame did not seek medical help. As a result, her health declined rapidly. She died in New York at the age of 57.

~

Dick Elliott (April 30, 1886-December 22, 1961)

Dick Elliott

Dick Elliott has one of those faces that you can almost place, and when you finally do, you recall that he is the uncredited actor on the porch in *It's a Wonderful Life* who urges George Bailey to, "Go ahead and kiss her. Oh. Youth is wasted on the wrong people!"

And if that voice is familiar then you may recall hearing Elliott as the man who played Mayor Pike in *The Andy Griffith Show*. But Elliott was also the judge recruited by Reginald Gardiner to perform the marriage ceremony for him and Barbara Stanwyck in another Christmas classic, *Christmas in Connecticut*.

Oh, yes. Dick Elliot is an everyman who was everywhere for a while.

Born Richard Damon Elliott, Dick Elliott played often in uncredited roles in over two hundred movies and was a popular character on many television shows. Because of his height and girth, Elliott played Santa Claus on TV shows, including for Red Skelton, Jack Benny, and Jimmy Durante.

Elliott was married to his long-time love Esther Claud from 1907-1949.

Born in Boston, Elliott died just before Christmas on December 22 in 1961 in Los Angeles from a heart-related illness.

Lionel Herbert Blythe Barrymore Apr 28, 1878-Nov 15, 1954

Lionel Barrymore as Mr. Potter

There's a pretty good chance you know actress Drew Barrymore (*Charlie's Angels)* better than you do her kinsman Lionel Barrymore. But like Ethyl Barrymore and John Barrymore (Drew's grandfather), Lionel is a significant contributor to American movie-making, and radio, too!

Barrymore first became well known in 1931 when he won the Academy Award for Best Actor in *A Free Soul.* After that, he returned to the public's attention in *It's a Wonderful Life.*

Riddled with arthritis later in his career, Barrymore relied upon pain shots and morphine to get through the day and could barely stand for any length of time. Barrymore still made some feel-good movies that audiences relished, such as *You Can't Take It With You.* He was featured as a crochety old man in nine

Dr. Kildare movies. Barrymore also appeared in *On Borrowed Time, Duel in the Sun,* and with Bogart and Bacall in *Key Largo.*

Barrymore was married twice, first to Doris Rankin, 1904-1922 and later to Irene Fenwick, 1923-1936.

Barrymore died on November 15, 1954 from a heart attack. His last role was a cameo appearance with his sister Ethyl in the movie, *Main Street to Broadway* in 1953.

Singalong with Mary and George in *It's a Wonderful Life:*

"Buffalo Gals," a favorite singalong song artfully used in *It's a Wonderful Life,* was written by John Hodges in 1844. The song's origins were in minstrel music, but were loved because you could adapt the lyrics to where you were living.

The lyric goes like this:

Buffalo gals won't you come out tonight?
Come out tonight
Come out tonight
Buffalo Gals won't you come out tonight?
and dance by the light of the moon.

The title of Buffalo gals refers—one supposes!-- to girls from Buffalo, New York. But you could use the name of any city or state where you are when you sing this hospitable lyric.
The reference to the light of the moon connects to the line that George Bailey says to Mary Hatch when they are strolling and he offers to lasso the moon for her. She replies brightly. "I'll take it. What's next?"

Your group might enjoy another Frank Capra movie.

It Happened One Night (1934)
Mr. Deeds Goes to Town (1936)
You Can't Take It With You (1938)
Meet John Doe (1941)
Mr. Smith Goes to Washington (1939)

Music connects the action in the next two movies that people enjoy watching during the holidays. The first movie, *Holiday Inn,* introduces the song "White Christmas," written by the man who didn't just influence American music. Many argue that songwriter Irving Berlin is American music.

Irving Berlin didn't lasso the moon, but he sure did lasso a piano.

SMALL TALK #3

#3 What'll I Do? A Story about Irving Berlin

Irving Berlin

Synopsis
Small Talk #3
"What'll I Do?" A Story about Irving Berlin

Type: Informative

Summary: Some music historians have asked how much influence Irving Berlin had on American music. The answer is most often: "Irving Berlin is American music." This Small Talk addresses Berlin's beginnings as a songwriter by talking about select Berlin songs and his love life.

Why I wrote this Small Talk: After reading a few books and particularly Mary Ellin Barrett's memoir of growing up as Berlin's daughter, I began to see how much influence Berlin had not only on music but American culture. But his story touched me too. A young widower, Berlin guarded his heart but fell in love with a rich young heiress whose father was against their marriage. Berlin's own music played in the background of their tortured love affair, that had, like his movies, a happy ending.

Why your group may want to sing after hearing this Talk: Most likely your audience members will know a great many of Berlin's songs. The memories of those lyrics will stir some powerful feelings and memories.

Tags: Irving Berlin, Ellin Mackay Berlin, minstrel music, Tin Pan Alley, Vaudeville, *Holiday Inn*, *White Christmas,* Bing Crosby, **Songs:** Always, Alexander's Ragtime Band, What'll I do?, Always

What you'll need: Ideally, a room with a piano and someone who can play Berlin's music. Or, access to a CD of Berlin's music with a connected speaker, or access to YouTube with a screen big enough for your audience to see some selected clips.

Talking Tip: If you have a way for Berlin's music to play while your group gathers, that will surely warm them up for the Talk. However, if your group likes to sing, choose a Berlin song and sing it together, either with accompaniment or acapella. "God Bless America" is always a great choice.

Small Talk #3
"What'll I do?" A story about Irving Berlin

From the time he was about eight years old (1896), Israel (Izzy) Baline, who would later be known as Irving Berlin, tried to earn money for his family and himself

A family of immigrants who escaped starvation from their home country somewhere in Russia, the eight-year-old Izzy did odd jobs for tips. The industrious boy sold newspapers on the streets of New York near the Hudson River.

One day, with his day's earnings in his hand, a heavy street crane knocked little Izzy into the river. A heroic stranger dove in and rescued the drowning boy. When they opened Izzy's clenched hand, the boy still held the few pennies he had earned that morning selling newspapers.

Those pennies were what stood between Izzy Baline and starvation.

Later, as he grew older, Izzy became a singing waiter

After selling newspapers Izzy became a song plugger, which was a genuine occupation in his day. Because there were few ways to introduce newly written music to potential customers, songwriters hired music pluggers to find a way to sing their songs where people could hear them. Some waiters sang for tips while they served the food.

While literally singing for his supper, Berlin taught himself to play the piano after hours. At first, he learned to play only the black keys. Berlin tinkered with notes and words, ultimately writing the first big success of his career, "Alexander's Ragtime Band." Relying upon a popular syncopated rhythm, the song struck a chord with people all over the world. The royalties launched Izzy Baline as a composer and a lyric writer. He also became known as Irving Berlin.

Irving Berlin begins writing music full-time

Because Irving was not a skilled pianist, he hired musical secretaries to transcribe the melodies he would plunk out on the keyboard and the words he wrote to go with them. Sometimes he would take the advice of his secretaries, like he did when Harry Ruby (later the other half of songwriting duo Kalmar and Ruby) advised Berlin not to release a certain song during WWI because there were already too many patriotic songs. So, Irving waited until WWII and finally gave the world, "God Bless America. Land that I love. Stand beside her. And guide her…."

Before Berlin offered his adopted country a song that rivals the national anthem in popularity, he gave us romantic ballads. They were written from a broken heart, for Irving married Dorothy Goetz in 1912, and his new young wife caught typhoid fever and died five months later.

A broken-hearted Berlin asks, "What'll I do?"

Berlin kept writing songs, but did not recover emotionally from that loss, writing the song that begins "What'll I do when you are far away and I am blue, what'll I do?"

That question was playing musically in the background of American life when the still young widower was invited to an upscale dinner party to fill in for someone who had cancelled. The hostess knew she could count on Irving to help fill out a dinner table when they needed another man. And Irving Berlin, who always preferred spontaneous plans to long-term ones, promptly said, yes.

Irving Berlin Meets Heiress Ellin Mackay

That night Berlin met the charming and very wealthy heiress Ellin Mackay, who, upon being introduced to him, said she loved his song, "What shall I do?"

"What'll I do?" Irving Berlin replied, giving her the exact title of the song.

"That's not very good grammar," Ellin said, mischievously.

Berlin accepted the flirtatious teasing gracefully, replying that he could use some help with his grammar. Irving and Ellin left the dinner party together and went out on the town for the rest of the evening where Berlin's music was playing here and there in various night clubs.

They danced. They sang. They talked. They fell in love.

Though love happened at first sight, theirs was not an easy courtship.

Ellin's father, a rich man, disapproved of his daughter dating a Jewish man. Ellin was Catholic. In the early 20th century in America, the two religions did not easily intermarry.

Mr. Mackay objects to Irving as a suitable suitor for his daughter

Discussions happened.

When accused of wanting to marry Ellin for her money, the now wealthy-in-his-own-right Irving Berlin replied that he would settle two million dollars on his bride the day they married.

That wasn't enough of an assurance for Mr. Mackay. He still objected, sending Ellin on a European trip to see if distance and time would cause her to forget Irving Berlin.

But Ellin couldn't forget Irving. She didn't want to forget him.

Upon her return to America, the couple struggled—stealing time to be together and then trying to stay apart.

Nothing worked.

Nineteen months later, Irving called Ellin early on a Monday morning, and didn't ask, 'What'll I do?" Berlin popped a different question. "Will you meet me at the courthouse right now and marry me?"

On her way to get her hair done, that rich girl was wearing a dress that needed to go to the dry cleaners. But she didn't stop to change her dress. Ellin hung up the phone, flew out the door, met Irving at the court house, and said, "I do."

"I do, too," Irving pledged, and to assure her of that, Berlin gave his bride a love song he had written for her, assigning all the rights to it as a first wedding present. That song begins "I'll be loving you, always." The year was 1926.

Irving Berlin promised Ellin Mackay that he would love her always

And that's the title of the song: "Always."

He did. She did. They loved each other deeply and for all of their long lives, but that didn't mean they didn't have their share of heartbreak. The couple had a child. Tragically, that baby boy died at Christmas; and though they had other children, Christmas for the Berlins was always a sad season of endurance and remembered sorrow.

Of course, their personal life did not stop them from celebrating Christmas, which was for Berlin an American holiday rather than a religious holiday. A famous couple, they obligingly posed for pictures for newspapers and magazines, and the poses were in front of the Christmas tree, the piano, or the fireplace where the stockings were hung.

Ellin Mackay Berlin hung her children's stockings with care

Stories were told of Ellin stuffing amazing Christmas stockings for their growing family. How did she get three stockings full and hung in time for the children to wake up and find them every year? The answer: Ellin Berlin had duplicate stockings made—empty ones to hang out on the fireplace and its twin already stuffed with gifts and ready to be exchanged for the empty ones once the children were asleep. Ellin Mackay Berlin was famously extravagant.

When criticism was offered about how freely his wife spent money, Berlin replied non-defensively, "I find it easier to make more money than to ask my darling to economize."

In this way, Irving Berlin revealed a great tenderness for those he loved, but he also asked them to be careful with his heart.

Crooner Bing Crosby sings for Berlin in *Holiday Inn*

In *Holiday Inn* you will hear that sweet entreaty when Bing (for Irving) sings a song to his love interest in the story played by Marjorie Reynolds. The song is "Be Careful, It's My Heart."

There is often a kind of plea that others be careful with his heart that runs through some of Berlin's most poignant love songs, like "How Deep is the Ocean," but you will also hear celebrations that fuel exuberant dancing, like "Cheek to Cheek" and "Steppin' Out With My Baby."

Berlin produced countless songs over time, and over time his wife Ellin turned to writing. She produced four well-received novels, showing them to her husband to read before she let them see the light of day. Berlin liked his wife's work, and the only advice he consistently gave her was, "Simplify. Simplify. Make it even simpler."

A great fan of and believer in the American vernacular, Berlin's lyrics, like his melodies, are simple—exquisitely simple. And because they are, they are imminently singable.

Some of Berlin's best-known musicals include: *Top Hat, Call Me Madam, Ziegfeld Follies, Annie Get Your Gun, Alexander's Ragtime Band, White Christmas, and Holiday Inn.*

Berlin wrote music for many years, living to a ripe old age of 101. In his later years, when he was living sequestered at home, most of his friendships were maintained over the telephone. That list of good friends had grown small, but for as long as they were alive, Berlin still chatted regularly with old friends like Harold Arlen, who passed away in 1986, and Fred Astaire who died in 1987.

When asked about his health near the end of his life, after he had outlived his beloved Ellin (she died 1988), Berlin replied with a twinkle, "If I'd known I was going to live this long, I would have taken better care of myself."

Irving Berlin died a year after he lost Ellin, in 1989. They were married for sixty-two years.

Ellin and Irving had four children. Their daughter Mary Ellin Barrett wrote a moving memoir of what it was like to grow up in the Berlin family. It is simply titled: *Irving Berlin: A Daughter's Memoir.*

It was a happy life, and Berlin's music, at times, buoyant and hopeful could also be mournful and melancholy. Almost always Irving Berlin's music tells a story about American life and how it feels to be in love.

SMALL TALK #4

#4 Irving Berlin's Holiday Inn

Bing Crosby and Marjorie Reynolds singing "White Christmas"

Synopsis
Small Talk #4
Irving Berlin's *Holiday Inn*

Type: Informative

Summary: A heart-warming story with a Christmas motif that relies upon the music of Irving Berlin to page through the calendar of holidays as viewers watch the good-natured rivalry between a singer and a dancer for a girl's affections.

Why I wrote this Small Talk: In its way *Holiday Inn* showcases many of the genres of American music, and I wanted to share that with others. From minstrel to ballads, the songs in *Holiday Inn* do more than chart the holidays on the calendar. They point to times in American music history that are the foundation of the Great American Songbook. In many ways, the movie is a musical history lesson. But it's so enjoyable we don't know that we are learning about our past.

Why your group will enjoy hearing more about Holiday Inn: Most likely your audience members love the songs, the story, and have grown older watching this movie. The biographies at the end of the Small Talk about Bing Crosby and the one about Fred Astaire should prove surprising and interesting. I hope you have time to include them in your presentation.

Tags: Bing Crosby, Fred Astaire, Marjorie Reynolds, Louise Beavers; **Songs:** Happy Holiday, Easter Parade, Be Careful, It's My Heart, White Christmas

What you'll need: The air date of the movie or a DVD or Blu Ray copy.

Additional Resources: This movie has been colorized in a new version and is available as a DVD or Blu-ray.

Note: Although considered primarily a Christmas movie, songs from *Holiday Inn* tie to months during the year with national holidays celebrated in song.

Songs in *Holiday Inn* by month
January "Let's Start the New Year Right"
February "Abraham"; the Valentine song, "Be Careful It's My Heart"; and "I Can't Tell a Lie"
April "Easter Parade"
July "Song of Freedom" & "Let's Say It with Firecrackers"
November "Happy Holiday" & "I've Got Plenty To Be Thankful For"
December "White Christmas" & "Happy Holiday/Holiday Inn"

~

Small Talk #4
Irving Berlin's *Holiday Inn*

Before Irving Berlin wrote his love song to the piano, "I love a Piano," many other people already felt the same way. Berlin loved a piano.

For a good long while the hallmark of a fine American home was having a piano in the living room. The purchase was a priority. Even very poor families had pianos because people loved to sing.

One person could usually play it.

Several people could tinker with it.

Everyone knew "Chopsticks," and everyone enjoyed "Chopsticks," and that includes the people who also played "Twinkle, Twinkle Little Star" and the duet version of "Heart and Soul. I fell in love with you....lost control."

The reason?

For a good while in the late 19th and early 20th century, everyone liked to sing.

In Berlin's day, everyone sang no matter how their voices sounded. Why not?

In the hey-day of people like Berlin who loved pianos, everyone sang.

Voices weren't judged for performance value or even if you could or couldn't carry a tune very well. Singing was just a different way of being together, of sharing a moment, some family time, and being part of the good-will gang gathered around the piano.

Singing is so very good for you

Listening to music is good for you, but singing especially uplifting songs is really good for you. Your brain lights up in all kinds of good ways when you listen to a song, sing a song, or play an instrument. Just tapping your toe to a beat is very good for your brain.   Singing, playing, and listening to music is good for your brain.

Music was good for Berlin, and he was good for music

Irving Berlin didn't let his self-consciousness about being an amateurish piano player keep him from writing music and the lyrics and often singing those songs himself.   Berlin had a thin, homey voice.

You can find Berlin singing his poignant prayer "God Bless America" on YouTube. You can find him singing "Oh, How I hate to Get Up in the Morning" on YouTube, too, and you can find his musicals playing year-round and can sing along.

The framework of *Holiday Inn* is a variety show

The story begins with two song-and-dance men explaining how they woo the ladies. Bing Crosby's character, Jim Hardy, does it with song. Fred Astaire's character, Ted Hanover, does it with dance.

The opening number is very engaging and sets up an ongoing storyline. These two very likable and talented men will sing and dance for a reward, and according to the song lyrics, a woman's affections is the prize.

But vying for the same girl is not the only tension that threads itself through *Holiday Inn* with scenes and action tied to the songs that Berlin has written to match holidays throughout the year.

Fred's Ted wants to dance more than Bing's Jim wants to sing. In fact, Jim wants to work less so he buys a farm and plans to take Ted's dance partner with him.

Lila Dixon, played charmingly by Virginia Dale, breezily loves Jim, but this big-city dancer doesn't want to live on the farm. Miss Lila likes the big city life and glamour. Homespun Jim finds out, leaves Lila behind to keep Ted romantic company, and goes on to his Connecticut farm. There, Jim discovers how much work farming is. He changes direction. He decides to convert the farm into a Holiday Inn, where entertainers only work on the holidays.

And that is the way that Irving Berlin is able to showcase the songs that he has written for Christmas and other holidays throughout the year.

The music supports the story and the holidays in Holiday Inn

Historically, musicals often had storylines that were interrupted by music which was injected or planted. But with *Holiday Inn,* the music supports the stories, and the dances do, too.

The musical numbers showcased in *Holiday Inn* that are written and staged by the character of Jim Hardy are elaborate, representing what has been before: burlesque shows, vaudeville shows, and minstrel shows.

The ways that public entertainment evolved in America happened in broad strokes like this: minstrel shows, Vaudeville, Broadway, and radio and movies emerged with the development of technology, which included microphones, speakers, and recording machines.

Minstrel acts were a kind of wide-ranging variety show

The February sketch in *Holiday Inn* celebrates Abraham Lincoln's *The Emancipation Proclamation*(1863) with the song "Abraham" and is performed in blackface. This cosmetic choice was common in Berlin's day (Crosby's, too, for *Holiday Inn* isn't the only early movie of his where Bing blacks up) Using burnt cork to blacken the face harkens back to minstrel shows that were still popular in the 40s but are now a touchstone of controversy. Minstrel shows had both black and white performers smearing their faces with burnt cork. It is unclear why or how this came into practice, but now using blackface is considered a form of mockery and disrespect.

Wearing blackface as make up on stage is not the only way minstrel music is characterized. Variety shows included all kinds of acts and all kinds of people. Minstrel shows often traveled by rail and on steamboats. You can read about more of this life in W. C. Handy's autobiography *Father of the Blues (1941)*. A native of Alabama, Handy was involved in minstrelsy in the early part of his career and shares his point of view in that book.

Vaudeville was very loose in format, using all kinds of acts—comedy and music

You will see acts in *Holiday Inn* that could have been played on a vaudeville stage. Once movies were invented, many performers from vaudeville were hired to use their acts on the screen. Once an act was captured in a movie, movie-goers stopped buying tickets to see vaudeville shows. So, it wasn't just the invention of technology that produced movies which put vaudeville acts out of business. When a vaudeville performer sold the act to use in a movie, anyone could see them sing, dance, juggle, perform magic tricks, or tell the same jokes anytime. No one needed to go to the vaudeville theatre to see them anymore. They could just go to the movies.

New York's Tin Pan Alley refers to various song plugger shops on W 28th Street between 5th and 6th Avenue

Famous people like George Gershwin, Bert Kalmar, and Harry Ruby all got their start on Tin Pan Alley. On that famous street, rows of offices for song writers and composers had pianos where song pluggers demonstrated music. They were so loud that passersby said it sounded like people were beating tin pans with spoons. But they were simply playing lots of cheap pianos very loudly at the same time. The street became famous about 1885, and its business mission—to plug songs--was made obsolete as technology produced wide-reaching radio, records, television—other mediums through which songs were introduced to the public.

Key songs from *Holiday Inn*

"White Christmas"(1942) Accounts vary about where this song was written, but the most prevalent is that Berlin was in California homesick and staring at a palm tree. The song "White Christmas" grew in popularity over time and because of the two Berlin Christmas movies. But more significantly, Bing Crosby sang this song repeatedly when he entertained the troops during WWII. The song connected with servicemen who took their affection for the song home with him. In the meantime, people at home keeping the home fires burning sang "White Christmas" as an anthem for when they would all be together again.

"Be Careful, It's My Heart" (1942) Used in the show for Valentine's Day, the ballad was predicted to become the favorite of the movie. The sentiment was true to Irving Berlin's guarded nature about love. His first wife died suddenly shortly after their marriage, and his grief caused him to be very cautious about pursuing any other love interests.

"Happy Holiday" (1942) Sung with so much activity in *Holiday Inn*, this song often gets overlooked, but it is a feel-good celebration of the season, including New Year's Eve.

"Easter Parade" (1933) In addition to the song "Easter Parade" in *Holiday Inn*, another movie bearing that song title as the movie's title featuring Judy Garland and Fred Astaire showcases this song.

~

Smaller Talking Points about the Players

The Players

Jim Hardy played by Bing Crosby
Ted Hanover played by Fred Astaire
Linda Mason played by Marjorie Reynolds
Mamie the cook played by Louise Beavers
Lila Dixon played by Virginia Dale

Bing Crosby (May 3, 1903-October 14, 1977)

Bing Crosby

You could just name some songs from the American songbook and have a pretty good idea of who Bing Crosby is. He sang most of them on his radio shows at one time or another. "White Christmas" isn't the only song Bing is famous for, and it wasn't his personal signature tune, which is, "Where the Blue of the Night Meets the Gold of the Day."

You may remember Crosby singing an Irish lullaby to the priest played by Barry Fitzgerald in *Going My Way*.

He sang Cole Porter's "True Love" with Grace Kelly on a boat in the remake of *The Philadelphia Story* called *High Society*.

Crosby playfully sang a rousing Johnny Mercer song, "The Waiter and the Porter and the Upstairs Maid" with Mary Martin. You can enjoy this song on YouTube.

In *Holiday Inn,* Crosby sang a Thanksgiving song that goes by so fast you don't really have time to absorb how good it is. The song is "I've Got a Lot to Be Thankful For." Fans of *White Christmas* tend to think first of "Count Your Blessings" as Berlin's signature Thanksgiving song, but there was another one in *Holiday Inn* that gets overlooked (mostly), and it's mighty pretty.

Want to list 20 more songs? It's easy to do.

But don't forget to add that Crosby was known for singing spontaneously what he refers to as a little spontaneous "Barbershop style" with people and friends and, well, soldiers and General Ike Eisenhower when he was entertaining the troops. Singing "barbershop" refers to a handful of people joining in to sing spontaneously and that included harmonizing in parts with the lead singer.

There's a story that General Eisenhower offered to help Crosby anyway he could while he was entertaining the troops. And Crosby asked for a car to use so that he could make a visit that wouldn't have been possible otherwise.

The General immediately loaned Crosby a vehicle and a driver. Afterwards, when Crosby returned, he asked Gen. Eisenhower if he could do anything for him. The General said something like, "When you get home, could you send me some grits?" General Eisenhower missed his hominy grits.

Upon his return to the United States, Crosby mentioned on his radio show that Gen. Eisenhower wanted some grits. Many good-hearted and sympathetic Southern women, who heard Crosby's radio broadcast, sent General Eisenhower so many pounds of grits that he contacted Crosby and asked him to turn off the grits supply.

Crosby did that, thanking the viewers on behalf of the General. That grits supply was the kind of proof that Crosby enjoyed a special relationship with his listeners and fans.

Crosby enjoyed a long fifty-year career, and his popularity never wavered. He started on the vaudeville stage, moved to radio, embraced improvements in performance styles brought by technological inventions, sang and acted in movies, earned an Oscar, made happy-go-lucky "Road" pictures with Bob Hope, and played as much golf as he could fit into his schedule.

At the age of 73, Crosby had just finished playing a good game of golf in Spain with new friends when on the way back to the locker room he collapsed. Medical help was called, but it couldn't save him. His second wife Kathryn was told the hard news. She said, "Tell everyone he had a good game of golf. He would love for that to be said about him."

Crosby was married twice, the first time to Dixie Lee in 1930. She died at the age of 42 in 1952. They had four sons together. He married Kathryn Grant in 1957, and they had three children together.

Crosby made 58 movies, hosted scores of radio programs, and traveled over 50,000 miles.

But here's a quick summary of Bing trivia:

Bing's given name: Harry Lillis Crosby, Jr.
Born where: Tacoma, Washington

How did he get the nickname Bing? It was from a favorite comic character he enjoyed as a kid.
Second-Best selling Christmas song: "Silent Night"
Crosby's favorite musician: Louis Armstrong   About Louis Armstrong, Crosby said: "He's the only musician who can't be replaced."
Frank Sinatra said of Crosby: "Crosby has the kind of voice that only happens in a lifetime. Why did he have to happen in mine?"
His favorite movie that he was in: *High Society*
Favorite Kind of Movie Crosby wanted to make: "My favorite kind of picture would be one that opened with a shot of me sitting in a rocking chair on a front porch. The rest of the picture would be what I saw..."
Bob Hope: How many "Road" pictures did he make with Bob Hope? Seven.
Academy Award: He won this Best Actor Award in 1944 for *Going My Way*.
Hats: He wore hats because he was balding, and he hated wearing his toupee.
Was Crosby Color Blind?: Because often his clothes didn't match in color, folks theorized that he must be color blind.
The Problem of Crosby's Ears: Yes, early in his career they tried to tape Crosby's protruding ears back, but Bing soon called a halt to it, and said, "Let 'em flap. They're mine."

For audience engagement:
Question: Can you name four accessories that were Bing's trademarks?
Answers: pipes, golf clubs, race horses, sports shirt

Actor/ Dancer: Fred Astaire (May 10, 1899-June 22, 1987)

Fred Astaire

In Robert Wagner's memoir *Pieces of My Heart: A Life* about his Hollywood days, the actor recalls seeing Fred Astaire wearing a brightly colored necktie for a belt. Wagner was impressed with Astaire's style, his panache.

Wagner may have thought that Astaire was styling, but the man who danced his weight off every time he made a movie was most likely trying to find something to hold up his pants.

Astaire always lost weight when making a movie. He dropped 20 pounds during the rehearsals for *Holiday Inn*. Bing Crosby said Astaire weighed in at 126 lbs. "You could spit through him," Crosby said, kind of enviously. (Crosby struggled with weight gain and was often teased about being portly.)

While Fred had a number of dancing partners, including Marjorie Reynolds in *Holiday Inn,* he is most famous for dancing with Ginger Rogers.

Professionally, he was often loosely referred to as Fred and Ginger; but in real life, Fred Astaire (Frederick Austerlitz) was a very happily married man, devoted to his first wife, and relished being known as 'Fred and Phyllis,' his wife of 21 years who died from lung cancer in 1954.

Upon his wife's death, Fred was inconsolable. Friends often found Astaire sitting off by himself sobbing into his hands. He was making a movie at the time of his grief, *Daddy Long Legs (1955)*, a romantic musical featuring Leslie Caron and some music of Johnny Mercer's. (You may recall that the *Daddy Long Legs* story was taken from Jean Webster's charming book by the same name)

Due to his great sorrow, Fred begged to be released from making the picture. He wasn't up to dancing or singing. Songwriter Johnny Mercer talked Astaire into staying. "The work will be good for you," Mercer promised. But then, Mercer knew something about heartbreak. (Recall that Mercer wrote Sinatra's classic gem, "One For My Baby." For *Daddy Long Legs*, Mercer wrote "Something's Gotta Give").

Astaire kept going—kept dancing. And the movie was a delight for audiences in spite of Astaire's grief while filming it.

Fred Astaire knew grief, but he also knew how to dance. He could sing winsomely and act. These gifts, groomed by skill and discipline, contradicted the discouraging assessment of a director after seeing an early Fred Astaire screen test. He wrote: "Astaire is balding. Can dance a little."

A lot of jokes have been made about that last commentary. Fred Astaire is, arguably, the most influential dancer in American history. Like songs, dance, too, should advance the storyline, and Astaire proved that in musical after musical, dancing not only with Ginger Rogers but also with Rita Hayworth and Eleanor Powell, of whom Astaire heartily approved. "Ginger couldn't really tap. But Eleanor could put down a step," said Fred.

Fred knew how to put down a step in some of the most innovative dance routines ever captured on film. Music critic Wilfrid Sheed said of his first viewing of Astaire's classic movie *Top Hat:* "I never recovered from seeing that movie."

There was something awe inspiring about the man who danced in tails and a top hat, an accessory that was chosen to make him look taller. Astaire hated tails and a top hat.

Fred preferred more casual elegance, and he and leading man Cary Grant were often assessed as the two most elegantly clad men in Hollywood.

Astaire's dancing was inspired by someone mostly forgotten: Mr. Bojangles, Bill Robinson.

The history of dance on Vaudeville, Broadway, and in movies ends up being allied significantly with the history of American music because of its integration of singing and dancing. Fred Astaire did both. Though retired, Astaire returned dramatically to the stage at the Oscar event in 1970. Bob Hope talked Fred Astaire into dancing for the audience. It was a hallmark moment for the 42nd Annual Academy Awards show when 71-year-old Fred Astaire cut loose. (You can see it on Youtube.)

But in his later years of not working or dancing regularly on TV or anywhere else, and with no one applauding, Fred Astaire was more likely to knock on the front door of Irving Berlin's house where a young girl who would later write a memoir of her father's life would say, "Hi, Mr. Astaire." And then turning, Irving's daughter Mary would call out, "Dad! Mr. Astaire is here."

And then Fred would go inside and find Irving waiting for him with a deck of cards. They sat opposite one another, snapping cards down in the particular rhythms of two iconic men who had made a significant contribution to music and cinema with sound and motion. They played gin rummy and swapped stories, the way retired people do.

Fred married Robyn Smith in 1980. They enjoyed seven years together before he died in 1987 from pneumonia at the age of 88.

Actress Louise Beavers (March 8, 1902-October 26, 1962)

Louise Beavers

Louise Beavers, the live-in cook at Holiday Inn, was not interested in being in movies at first. The only films she had ever seen with black people featured them as savages. Sweet-tempered Louise Beavers didn't want to play a savage.

But producers didn't want Mrs. Beavers to play savages either. Because of her "pleasing personality," they wanted Ms. Beavers to play roles of service--mammies and maids. When derided by others for making her living this way, Beavers replied, "I play the part. I don't live it."

She provided a breakout performance in the 1934 version of Fannie Hurst's story *Imitation of Life*. There, the problems of being black in America were explored persuasively and dramatically. (Another version of this movie was made in 1959 with Lana Turner, and Juanita Moore effectively played the role that Beavers had first introduced.)

Mrs. Beavers' long and acclaimed career includes work in radio and an early television sitcom *Beulah* featuring black actors. When Hattie McDaniel fell ill with breast cancer, Beavers took over the role. Later, Mrs. Beavers played a maid on the first two seasons of *The Danny Thomas Show*.

Beavers was married twice, the first time to Robert Clark and later to Leroy Moore to whom she was married when she died of a heart attack in 1962 in Los Angeles at the age of 60.

Marjorie Reynolds (Aug 12, 1917-Feb 1, 1997)

Marjorie Reynolds

Bing Crosby had Peter Pan star Mary Martin in mind for the role of Linda Mason when he agreed to perform in *Holiday Inn*. But Mary Martin was pregnant, and other obligations developed that prevented her from taking the role.

Tryouts happened, and Marjorie Reynolds was up for the second female lead Lila Dixon. The tryout stretched out for eighteen long hours. And because Reynolds didn't complain and was talented, she was hired, but not for the second female lead—for the first, Linda Mason-- Bing Crosby's love interest.

Born Marjorie Goodspeed on August 12, 1917, Marjorie took her first dance lessons at age 4. She was part of the early growth of silent movies, but she is most famous for her role as Linda Mason in *Holiday Inn,* where her dancing skills are showcased opposite Fred Astaire. Marjorie's voice is dubbed, and the songs are sung by Martha Mears.

Though most famous for her role in *Holiday Inn,* Reynolds also played Peg Riley opposite William Bendix in *The Life of Riley* and made other appearances on popular television shows like *Leave it to Beaver* and *The Millionaire.*

Marjorie married twice, and Reynolds is the last name of her first husband. They had one child, Linda. Marjorie died on February 1, 1997 of congestive heart failure while walking her dog.

SMALL TALK #5

#5 Irving Berlin's White Christmas

Bing Crosby and Danny Kaye in *White Christmas*

Synopsis
Small Talk #5
Irving Berlin's White Christmas

Type: Informative or Interactive

Summary: Often referred to as a sequel to *Holiday Inn*, this glamorous feel-good musical does not take up where any storyline in the first movie to use the song "White Christmas" left off. Rather, it is a movie with variety shows built in to use Berlin's music, and these commonalities are delightful.

Why I wrote this Small Talk: The truth is, I usually have this movie playing in the background while I make my annual Christmas fudge. From the signature song "White Christmas" to "Sisters" to "Snow" to "The Best Things Happen While You're Dancing" there simply isn't a better Christmas soundtrack to keep you company while you're either watching it absorbed or busy with card writing, present wrapping, or cooking.

Why your group will engage with this Small Talk: The four primary characters all had interesting lives, and their biographies tell some of each person's story. Danny Kaye was routinely fired from early jobs, finally becoming a comedian. Vera-Ellen lost a baby and retired from performing afterwards. Rosemary Clooney had a disappointing love affair with music arranger Nelson Riddle, which may partially explain why "Love You Didn't Do Right By Me" was her favorite song in the movie. And Bing Crosby was named after a cartoon he loved. So why wouldn't your group, who most likely loves this movie, enjoy this Talk?

Special Message: The biography of Bing Crosby at the back of this Small Talk on *White Christmas* is the same biography at the back of *Holiday Inn*. It's big enough to just use part of it one time and the rest of it the next time if your group hears both Talks this year.

Tags: Players: Bing Crosby, Danny Kaye, Rosemary Clooney, Vera-Ellen, Dean Jagger, Mary Wickes; **Songs**: Sisters, Snow, Count Your Blessings, White Christmas

What you'll need: This movie often runs for whole days at a time during the holidays. In short, it's hard to miss! However, if you can't catch an air date, then a DVD or access to direct demand is needed.

Ice Breaker: At the beginning of this movie, Betty (Rosemary Clooney) says her brother is out of the country. Which state does she mention, and when did it become a state?

The answer: She mentions Alaska, which became a state in 1959. The movie *White Christmas* was made in 1954.

Small Talk #5
Irving Berlin's White Christmas

For all of the red velvet, snow, and glamour in *White Christmas*, the best moment in the movie is at the very beginning when, if you listen very closely, Bing Crosby sings the title song "White Christmas" almost acapella.

Sure.

Danny Kaye playing the role of Phil Davis is sitting on the stage below him cranking what looks like a phonograph but sounds like a big music box that plays an accompanying piece of music. Crosby carries the melody, his voice sweet and true, like his gaze.

There's a reason that rendition is so touching. One can only imagine that Bing Crosby, who flew thousands of miles in real life singing it to active duty soldiers, was reliving the stripped-down way he had to perform for soldiers gathered loosely around the back of a truck where he might stand and sing or, in the movie, a hastily contrived platform while overhead enemy planes are flying.

The men in the movie are about to say so-long to their general who has been reassigned. And soon, General Waverly, ably played by Dean Jagger, appears and gives them the kind of pep talk with a kick in the pants that sounds like the old guard saying good-bye, covering the sad sentiment of leaving when he doesn't want to go.

Bing (Bob) and Danny (Phil) and the men give General Waverly a rousing send-off with a song that encourages him on his way:

"We'll follow the old man wherever he wants to go...."

It's a good moment in the movie, with the general riding off in a jeep only to be met again sometime later after the war, when Bob and Phil have become a successful pair of entertainers. When they see the "Old Man" again, he has retired from military service and is trying to run a Holiday Inn in Vermont.

The four main characters head to Vermont for the snow

Bing and Danny—Bob Wallace and Phil Davis—accompany the Haynes sisters, played by Rosemary Clooney and Vera-Ellen on a train, ostensibly to see the celebrated snow; but there isn't any.

No snow means trouble

And that's trouble for the Holiday Inn owner, who is about to go broke.

Bob and Phil decide to bring their show to him and call the guys from their old unit together for a great musical boost of encouragement that may also bring the General some much needed business—paying guests!

But that goal takes some rocky and romantic turns, and along the way Bing sings some more. And so does Rosemary Clooney, who plays Betty Haynes. Vera-Ellen, playing her sister Judy Haynes, lip syncs; and if you listen closely, particularly to the "Sisters" number you will hear that Rosemary has sung both parts, dubbing (subbing?) for Vera-Ellen.

For the movie, Vera-Ellen had trouble singing. Rosemary had trouble dancing. They made it happen anyway, playing their parts in what is one of the most visually pleasing spectacle movies about the season featuring Irving Berlin's music.

Lovely moments occur

When Betty finds herself unable to sleep because of stirred up feelings for Bob (Bing), she goes looking for a glass of buttermilk in the main lodge. She finds Bob instead. Hearing she can't sleep, he serenades her with "When you're worried and you can't sleep. Count your blessings instead of sheep...." a song that functions as a lullaby and was most likely inspired as a monologue by composer Irving Berlin, who was a famous worrier and insomniac.

The classic formula of a love story within a musical continues. Boy meets girl. They like each other. Confusion happens. They separate. The problem gets straightened out. Boy gets girl.

A King and Queen come calling

After the final scene, with the big Christmas tree lit up and the snow falling, had been shot, the King and Queen of Greece came calling and asked to see a scene of the movie being shot.

It was too late! The movie was finished. But no one told them that. Instead, the director, Michael Curtiz, called the actors back to work to re-enact the final scene. Everyone except Bing Crosby obliged. He had a golf game scheduled, and he wasn't giving that up just to sing for the King and a Queen. Bing asked his buddy Rosemary to cover for him. "I'm going over the wall," he said.

And Bing went over the wall, spending as little time as possible trying to impress anyone because, life is precious. He knew that.

So did Irving Berlin, who, Rosemary recalls in her memoir, came over and stood with her in the shadows and quietly held her hand while one of the scenes was being filmed.

A faithful husband to wife Ellin, Irving only took sweet Rosemary's hand because it was a moment of shared tenderness while something lovely was happening in front of them, and they were witnessing it together.

That's probably as good a way as any for someone to settle down on the couch with a glass of something—maybe buttermilk-- and watch while Danny, Bing, Vera, and Rosemary prove that "The best things happen while you're dancing"—and while you're singing. And while it's snowing.

Listen for an early Berlin song "Blue Skies" at the beginning performed quite differently than it is offered elsewhere, and before that, maybe just a hint of "Abraham" in the beginning, a nod to *Holiday Inn*. For the elements that link the two movies have about as much to do with a nod as anything, but the nods are significant and worth holding someone else's hand to share the good time that is always enjoyed with this experience of a musical white Christmas.

Small Talking Points about the Players

The Players

Bob Wallace played by Bing Crosby
Phil Davis played by Danny Kaye
Betty Haynes played by Rosemary Clooney
Judy Haynes played by Vera-Ellen
Emma Allen the housekeeper played Mary Wickes
General Tom Waverly played by Dean Jagger

Bing Crosby (May 3 1903-October 14, 1977)
This brief biographical sketch is the same one included in Small Talk #4: Irving Berlin's Holiday Inn

You could just name some songs from the American songbook and have a pretty good idea of who Bing Crosby is. He sang most of them on his radio shows at one time or another. "White Christmas" isn't the only song Bing is famous for, and it wasn't his personal signature tune, which is, "Where the Blue of the Night Meets the Gold of the Day."

You may remember Crosby singing an Irish lullaby to the priest played by Barry Fitzgerald in *Going My Way*.

He sang Cole Porter's "True Love" with Grace Kelly on a boat in the remake of *The Philadelphia Story* called *High Society*.

Crosby playfully sang a rousing Mercer song, "The Waiter and the Porter and the Upstairs Maid," with Mary Martin. You can enjoy that on YouTube.

In *Holiday Inn,* Crosby sang a Thanksgiving song that goes by so fast you don't really have time to figure out how good it is. The song is "I've Got a Lot to Be Thankful For." Fans of *White Christmas* tend to think first of "Count Your Blessings" as Berlin's signature Thanksgiving song, but there was another one in this movie that gets overlooked (mostly), and it's mighty pretty.

Want to list 20 more songs? It's easy to do.

But don't forget to add that Crosby was known for singing spontaneously what he refers to as a little spontaneous "Barbershop style" with people and friends and, well, soldiers and Ike Eisenhower when he was entertaining the troops. Singing "barbershop" refers to a handful of people joining in to sing spontaneously and that included harmonizing in parts with the lead singer.

There's a story that Eisenhower offered to help Crosby anyway he could while he was entertaining the troops. And Crosby asked for a car to use so that he could make a visit that wouldn't have been possible otherwise.

The General immediately loaned Crosby his own vehicle and the driver. Afterwards, when Crosby returned, he asked Gen. Eisenhower if he could do anything for him. The General said something like, "When you get home, could you send me some grits?" General Eisenhower missed his hominy grits.

Upon his return to the United States, Crosby mentioned that Gen. Eisenhower wanted some grits on his radio show, and many Southern women, who heard Crosby's radio broadcast, sent General Eisenhower so many pounds of grits that he contacted Crosby and asked him to turn off the grit supply.

He did, thanking the viewers on behalf of the General. That grit supply was the kind of proof that Crosby enjoyed a special relationship with his listeners and fans.

Crosby enjoyed a long fifty-year career, and his popularity never wavered. He started on the Vaudeville stage, moved to radio, embraced improvements in performance style brought by technological inventions, sang and acted in movies, earned an Oscar, made happy-go-lucky "Road" pictures with Bob Hope, and played as much golf as he could fit into his schedule.

At the age of 73, Crosby had just finished playing a good game of golf in Spain with new friends when on the way back to the locker room he collapsed. Medical help was called, but it couldn't save him. His second wife Kathryn was told the hard news. She said, "Tell everyone he had a good game of golf. He would love for that to be said about him."

Crosby was married twice, the first time to Dixie Lee in 1930. She died at the age of 42 in 1952. They had four sons together. He married Kathryn Grant in 1957, and they had three children together.

Crosby made 58 movies, hosted scores of radio programs, and traveled over 50,000 But here's a quick summary of Bing trivia:

Bing's given name: Harry Lillis Crosby, Jr.

Born where: Tacoma, Washington

How did he get the nickname Bing? It was from a favorite comic character he enjoyed as a kid.

Second-Best selling Christmas song: "Silent Night"

Crosby's favorite musician: Louis Armstrong Of Armstrong, Crosby said: "He's the only musician who can't be replaced."

Frank Sinatra said of Crosby: "Crosby has the kind of voice that only happens in a lifetime. Why did he have to happen in mine?"

His favorite movie that he was in: *High Society*

Favorite Kind of Movie Crosby wanted to make: "My favorite kind of picture would be one that opened with a shot of me sitting in a rocking chair on a front porch. The rest of the picture would be what I saw…"

Bob Hope: How many "Road" pictures did he make with Bob Hope? Seven.

Academy Award: He won this Best Actor Award in 1944 for *Going My Way*.

Hats: He wore hats because he was balding, and he hated wearing his toupee.

Was Crosby Color Blind? Because often his clothes didn't match in color, folks theorized that he must be color blind.

The Problem of Crosby's Ears: Yes, early in his career they tried to tape Crosby's protruding ears back, but Bing soon called a halt to it, and said, "Let 'em flap. They're mine."

For audience engagement:
Question: Can you name four accessories that were Bing's trademarks?
Answers: pipes, golf clubs, race horses, sports shirt

~

Danny Kaye (January 18, 1911-March 3, 1987)

Danny Kaye

Although not primarily a dancer, Danny Kaye was so agile that he could dance. He was the third person asked to play the role of Phil Davis in *White Christmas*. Fred Astaire couldn't take the role. Donald O'Conner said *yes* and then backed out. And finally, Danny Kaye was asked, and he eagerly said *yes*.

Born David Daniel Kaminsky in Brooklyn, Danny Kaye was a man of great many interests. He left school early and held a number of different jobs, most often getting fired. A dentist hired Kaye to look after his office and run errands for him. The dentist fired Danny Kaye for using his expensive dentist's drill on the office woodwork. Kaye later married the daughter of the irate dentist whose drill he ruined--Sylvia Fine.

A series of other odd jobs followed with about as much success.

In 1933, Kaye joined a vaudeville act that went on the road and ultimately to Asia. Because of the language barriers, Kaye was not understood by the audience, and he began to pantomime what a song was trying to say. The audience loved Kaye's zany pantomimes and that reputation and skill helped him kickstart his acting career when he returned home to the United States.

Kaye went from Broadway to movies and ultimately to having his own television show from 1963-67.

In his later years, he loved baseball, aviation, and cooking, installing a sophisticated Chinese kitchen in the alley behind his house.

Kaye's love interest in *White Christmas* is played by Vera-Ellen. It is the second time they shared the screen together. The first movie was *Wonder Man* (1945).

Kaye died at the age of 76 from heart failure.

Rosemary Clooney (May 23, 1928-June 29, 2002)

Rosemary Clooney and Bing Crosby in "White Christmas"

Rosemary Clooney was grateful for Bing Crosby's recruitment of her for the Christmas extravaganza, *White Christmas*.

"I was supposed to sing and dance in the movie, and I'm not a good dancer," she admitted in her memoir *Girl Singer*. It took her forever to learn the modest routine for the sisters' act, and Vera-Ellen, a highly skilled dancer, grew bored with Rosemary's clumsy efforts and let her double stand in while Rosemary rehearsed. It all worked out fine, however, because Vera-Ellen couldn't sing very well. Rosemary sang both parts in the song "Sisters" and Vera-Ellen lip synced to Rosemary's vocals.

Rosemary was born in Kentucky and began singing after she and her real sister Betty were left alone by their mother to fend for themselves. The girls started as a sister act, but over time Rosemary's voice took her into a one-woman act.

"My favorite song in the movie wasn't "White Christmas," said Rosemary. "It was "Love, You Didn't Do Right by Me."

Rosemary sang that song with conviction. Clooney married her first husband, Jose Ferrer, twice before his infidelity became something she couldn't live with after all.

Later, she fell in love with her favorite music arranger, Nelson Riddle, who promised to leave his wife for her, but he never did. She asked Frank Sinatra to intercede on her behalf one day over lunch, for Nelson Riddle arranged much of Frank's music, too. Sinatra dismissed the personal request and warned Rosemary, "The pills you are taking are hurting your voice."

They were, Rosemary agreed, as she admits in her autobiography. And ultimately the drugs derailed her career and caused her to try and relaunch it later after she was clean and sober.

In 1997, she married long-time love, Dante DiPaolo, and continued singing publicly.

In 2001, Clooney performed in Hawaii, singing one of Berlin's best-known songs, "God Bless America." She died the next year from lung cancer in 2002.

~

Vera-Ellen (Feb 16, 1921-Aug 30, 1981)

Danny Kaye and Vera-Ellen dancing in "White Christmas"

In *White Christmas,* the best things happen while you're dancing, and in that movie Vera-Ellen dances with the limber and likable Danny Kaye.

The hyphenated name was given to her by her mother, who saw it in a dream. That name became famous on the stage and in movies, most famously *White Christmas.*

But before *White Christmas*, Vera-Ellen appeared in a biopic of Kalmar and Ruby's musical partnership, *Three Little Words* and also in *The Belle of New York.*

Like many big screen actresses, Vera-Ellen made the transition to being a guest star on television variety shows hosted by popular performers of the day, including Perry Como and the first lady of TV in her day, Dinah Shore.

Because of her extreme thinness, many believed that Vera-Ellen had an eating disorder like anorexia, but close family members said, no. Vera Ellen danced, took dancing lessons all her life, and was an avid swimmer, which, they argued, were the reasons she stayed so thin.

She was married first to Robert Hightower in 1941. The couple divorced in 1946. Later Vera Ellen married Victor Rothschild in 1954. They had a daughter together. After the death of the daughter from SIDS at three months old, Vera Ellen retired from performing. The couple divorced in 1966.

She died at the age of sixty from ovarian cancer.

Dean Jeffries Jagger (November 7, 1903- Feb 5, 1991)

Dean Jagger

Born in Lima, Ohio, in 1903, the future Academy Award winner for best supporting actor in *12 O'clock High*, had a difficult time staying in school. He wanted to act, and practiced his speaking skills with the cows on the farm where he grew up.

Practice paid off for Jagger.

The year after *White Christmas*, Jagger played opposite Spencer Tracy in *Bad Day at Black Rock*.

Other popular movies include *The Nun's Story (1959)*, *Executive Suite(1954)*, *Parrish,*(1961) *Cash McCall*, (1960) *Elmer Gantry (1960),* and *Firecreek*.

Jagger was married three times.

He died in his sleep at age 87 in California.

Mary Wickes (June 13, 1910 -October 22, 1995)

Mary Wickes

Is she the actress who played the Wicked Witch of the West? No! That was Margaret Hamilton.

Mary Wickes usually plays a wise-cracking supporting character who sometimes nudges the main character in a better direction. That's not true to the role Wickes plays in *White Christmas,* however, where she shoves sweet Rosemary Clooney away from good-guy Bing Crosby when everyone watching knew that the guy was a keeper.

Wickes' unfortunate miscommunication in that role is unusual. More often, she's the chummy and helpful sidekick as she is to Bette Davis in the classic coming of age story, *Now, Voyager.* She appeared in *Dear Heart* (1964), *Good Morning, Miss Dove* (1955), and *The Music Man* (1962).

Born Mary Isabella Wickenhauser, Wickes became an adept comedian and a popular guest star on TV variety shows, starring with Lucille Ball and Doris Day.

She died from complications with hip surgery in 1995 at the age of 85.

SMALL TALK #6

#6 Miracle on 34th Street

Edmund Gwenn, Natalie Wood, and Maureen O'Hara

Synopsis
Small Talk # 6
Miracle on 34th Street (1947)

Type: Informative

Summary: Tapping into the mythical story of Santa Claus, who delivers gifts to children all around the world on Christmas Eve, a theme in *Miracle on 34th Street* challenges cynical people to reconsider the value of believing in what common sense says is not possible.

Why I wrote this Small Talk: Edmund Gwenn's performance is why I find this movie so entertaining. Too, after reading Maureen O'Hara's memoir **'Tis Herself,** I was surprised to learn that the movie was filmed during a very cold winter in New York and that the 1946 Macy's Parade was the actual parade we see in this movie. They had to work fast in the cold to get those early shots. Too, who doesn't love character actress Thelma Ritter, and this was her first movie performance.

Why your group will enjoy this Small Talk: It may have been a while since your group watched this movie, because it's not always a regular annual choice. But I watched it again to write this Small Talk, and I was impressed with the deft humor, the homage to shared humanity, and the artful swipes at wrong-headed psychology, which often gets overlooked. It's great fun!

Tags: Maureen O'Hara, Natalie Wood, John Payne, Edmund Gwenn, Thelma Ritter, Macy's Department Store

What you'll need: The air date for Miracle on 34th Street (1947) or a DVD or Blu-Ray copy.

Ice Breaker: If you did believe in Santa Claus, what would you ask for this year?

Small Talk #6
Miracle on 34th Street

You don't notice Maureen O'Hara's trademark deep auburn hair in the black and white classic *Miracle on 34th Street*. Her character's name is Doris Walker, and she is stressfully directing the Macy's Christmas parade. That's the genuine Macy's Parade of 1946 in the movie. New York City was bitterly cold that morning, and the crew and actors only had a brief chance at getting one good shot for each scene. Macy's wasn't going to hold up its parade for movie-making!

So, O'Hara and Edmund Gwenn, who played Kris Kringle, were trying to stay warm while they got the scene right. He did. She did.

And that included the troublesome moment in the movie when the Santa that Doris (Maureen) had hired to ride in the Macy's sleigh float was too inebriated to do the job. A witness to this disgraceful event, Kris Kringle, standing nearby, is shocked!

Doris hires Kris Kringle on the spot to take the drunk Santa's place, and he proves himself to be a natural driving a reindeer-drawn sleigh float and, later, when he takes the job permanently to hear children tell him what they want for Christmas, he is graciousness itself.

But why shouldn't he be?

The bearded man believes he is the real Kris/Santa. Right away when he is welcoming children, Kris has a memorable exchange with a child's mother played by Thelma Ritter in her first screen role.

Her child wants something that Macy's doesn't have. And Kris tells her where she can find it—another department store.

Ritter (no character name in the movie) is touched by that helpful response, and so are other parents.

A new holiday advertising campaign is launched!

Because of Kris' example, Macy's begins helping people find what they need for Christmas, even if it is only available at another store. Customers of Macy's love the idea and consider it an anti-commercialism stance. And it is. But behind this theme of de-commercializing Christmas is the position of Doris, the mother who doesn't teach her child to believe in Santa Claus and what he stands for: believing in the impractical.

The word that gets defined in the context of the story is faith. But that word "faith" here is not a stance about God or the religious aspects of Christmastime. It's more about learning to pretend and living imaginatively and kindly.

This end result is worked out in a courtroom where Kris Kringle is put on trial and set up to prove that he is the real Santa Claus. His lawyer, Fred Gailey, played effectively by John Payne, is inspired to have the children's letters addressed to Santa being held at the post office brought to the courtroom. His motive? When a federal agency recognizes Kris Kringle as Santa, that is legal proof enough.

But that tidy piece of plot business does not take the place of the emotional growth of Doris Walker's daughter Susan (played by Natalie Wood), who, in a leap of faith, confides to Kris Kringle that she wants a house to live in with a back yard. (She and her single mom live in an apartment.)

On their way home from the successful courtroom experience where Kris is validated legally, young Susan sees the house she has imagined and demands they stop the car. While the courtroom business has tidily and delightfully concluded, the additional find of a highly desired home adds a layer of wonder to the story.

It was another bitterly cold day!

O'Hara said it was another cold day when they filmed that last scene at the child's desired dream house—as cold as it was on the day they shot the scenes with the Macy's parade. It was so cold that the cameras froze.

A lady who lived across the street from the house they were using as the set brought them all in to her house to thaw out. O'Hara said that moment was like so many others when the kindness of nearby people felt like the real miracle wrought by the movie.

Miracle on 34th Street was a hit!

While the players thought it was going to be a popular movie, they didn't expect it to become a classic. But over time, the audience has continued to grow, and O'Hara has continued to answer questions about it:

"Was that the real Mr. Macy playing himself in the movie?"

"No." said O'Hara. "That man's name is actor Harry Antrim."

But her favorite question to be asked is:

"Are you the lady who knows Santa Claus?"

O'Hara always answered brightly, "Yes, I am. What would you like me to tell him?"

Small Talking Points about the Players

The Players
Doris Walker played by Maureen O'Hara
Susan Walker, the daughter, played by a very young Natalie Wood
Fred Gailey the lawyer and romantic interest for Doris played by John Payne
Kris Kringle played by Edmund Gwenn
Child's Mother played by Thelma Ritter

Maureen O'Hara (August 17, 1920- October 24, 2015)

Maureen O'Hara

Perhaps you have a favorite Maureen O'Hara movie. Maybe you love the feel-good flick with John Wayne *McLintock!(1963)* or their other enduring classic *The Quiet Man (1952)*. Or maybe your first thought was of that delightful movie where Hayley Mills played two roles as twin sisters: *The Parent Trap* (1961) and O'Hara played her mother. And then there's that heart-tugging movie with Henry Fonda, *Spencer's Mountain* (1963) -- the movie that inspired the television series *The Waltons*. You might even recall seeing O'Hara in another holiday movie *The Christmas Box* (1995).

But before O'Hara made any of those movies, she starred in *Miracle on 34th Street*.

It was one of her favorite working experiences, and she recalled in her memoir, *'Tis Herself,* how she enjoyed strolling with Edmund Gwenn and John Payne down New York's 5th Avenue after the day's work was done, window shopping together. Natalie Wood couldn't go with them. It was past her bedtime!

O'Hara recalls the time as one of great fellowship, friendships made, and much talk about making a sequel. But that never happened.

O'Hara was married three times. The first marriage was annulled. The second one to Will Price lasted ten years, but his alcoholism caused its demise.

Her third marriage to General Charles F. Blair Jr., lasted until his death in 1978.

In addition to acting and writing her best-selling memoir, O'Hara loved to sing, and called singing her "first love." She appeared on the Perry Como and Andy Williams variety television shows, among others.

Maureen O'Hara died in her sleep from natural causes at the age of 95.

~

Natalie Wood (July 20, 1938-November 29, 1981)

Natalie Wood

Natalie Wood began her acting career playing the eight-year-old daughter of Doris Walker in *Miracle on 34th Street*. O'Hara loved Natalie as a daughter, and called her affectionately "Natasha."

Wood's parents were Russian immigrants, and her given name was Natalia.

She quickly gained fame in *Rebel Without a Cause* and later playing love-torn Maria in *West Side Story*. She also portrayed the poignant love experience of a young woman in *Splendor in the Grass* and later, *Love with the Proper Stranger*.

In addition to drama, Wood had a knack for comedy and played a winsome thief in *Penelope*.

Married twice to television actor Robert Wagner, she died mysteriously in a drowning accident at the age of 43.

John Payne (May 23, 1912-December 6, 1989)

John Payne

John Payne is best known for *Miracle in 34th Street* where he plays the lawyer who defends Kris Kringle in court. A gifted actor and affable, attractive man, he often played a love interest as he did in the movie *Tin Pan Alley* (1940) with Alice Faye.

After a horrific traffic accident that required two years to recover, Payne appeared on television, and his last role was with Peter Falk in a Columbo episode: *Forgotten Lady*.

He was married first to Anne Shirley (1937-1943) and later to Gloria De Haven (1944-1950). Both marriages ended in divorce. In 1953, he married Alexandra Crowell Curtis.

John Payne died of congestive heart failure in 1989 at the age of 77.

Edmund Gwenn (Edmund John Kellaway) Sept 26, 1877-Sept 6, 1959

Edmund Gwenn

Edmund Gwenn won the Academy Award for Best Supporting Actor in 1947 because as he does in the movie, in real life he made people believe he was Kris Kringle. Was it the twinkle in his eye or his Santa-esque beard that before going to sleep he fluffs over the blanket? You have to watch the movie for yourself to see your own clues about what makes Gwenn one of the most lovable and watchable characters in any movie-- and especially *Miracle on 34th Street.*

British born, Gwenn moved to California, where his career thrived. Fans enjoy his work in a variety of popular movies, including *Apartment for Peggy* (1948), *Cheers for Miss Bishop (1941), and Les Misérables* (1952).

He was married to Minnie Terry in 1901, and divorced in 1916. He never married again. Gwenn died of pneumonia just before his 82nd birthday.

Thelma Ritter   (February 14, 1902-February 5, 1969)

Thelma Ritter

If you have seen the Hitchcock classic *Rear Window* (1954), then you know that Thelma Ritter can steal a scene from leading man Jimmy Stewart and leading lady, the well-dressed Grace Kelly.

And if you have seen *All About Eve* (1950), you witnessed her take one line and steal the scene from Betty Davis.

And if you really enjoy old movies you saw Ritter get suddenly rich in the movie *Lucy Gallant* (1955) with Jane Wyman and start dressing better. In *The Mating Season* (1951) she went broke and ditched the bankrupt family business-- a hamburger stand-- to join her son and his newlywed wife.

In *Pillow Talk* (1959) with Doris Day and Rock Hudson, Ritter drank too much but not so much she didn't steal scenes from Doris, too.

Ritter was nominated for Best Supporting Actress six times, more than any other actor. Director Frank Capra said Thelma Ritter was the finest supporting actress he had ever known.

Ritter married Joseph Moran in 1927, and the couple had two children. Brooklyn born Thelma Ritter died in New York of a heart attack just before turning 67.

SMALL TALK #7

#7 I Love to Whistle!

Synopsis
Small Talk #7
I Love to Whistle

Type: Informative and Interactive

Summary: Once upon a time whistling occurred as a natural and playful part in movies and television shows. From accompanying a song to calling your horse, whistling was a way of communicating, often teasingly, flirtatiously, and discreetly. If you haven't whistled or even thought about it in a while, this Talk reminds you to "Pucker up, Buttercup."

Why I wrote this Small Talk: I became aware of how much Bing Crosby whistles in addition to singing, not only in *Holiday Inn* but in other performances, such as his medley duet with Mary Martin that includes the song "I Love to Whistle." You can find that delightful medley on YouTube.

Why your group will enjoy this Small Talk: If the members of your audience have ever whistled along with Andy Griffith's theme song, elbowed someone when Gene Autry whistled for his horse Champion, or grinned when Lauren Bacall flirted with her future husband Humphrey Bogart, they will enjoy whistling down memory lane with this Talk.

Tags: Fats Waller, Gene Autry, Champion the Wonder Horse, *The Andy Griffith Show's* theme song, Lauren Bacall, Humphrey Bogart, Mary Martin, Bing Crosby, I Love Lucy, Rock Hudson

What you'll need: Puckered lips, maybe a little Chapstick, and a sense of humor

Ice Breaker Question:

Which Alfred Hitchcock movie used whistling as part of its signature song "Que Sera Sera"?

The answer for you: *The Man Who Knew Too Much* (1956) with Jimmy Stewart and Doris Day

The YouTube video of that song and the whistling can be enjoyed. Find the address at the back of this book.

Small Talk #7
I Love to Whistle

Did you grow up whistling?

Do you know a whistler?

Some people do it unconsciously, and that kind of repetitive mindless whistling can be annoying. The "I Love Lucy" show demonstrated this in season 4 with the Palm Springs episode. Rock Hudson shows how mindless whistling can get on someone's nerves. It's a funny scene using whistling to represent the kind of unconscious behaviors that can annoy people. Whistling can be that. Or whistling can be another way of communicating.

Cowboy Gene Autry called Champion the Wonder Horse with a whistle.

Indians about to attack a barricaded fort signaled each other a distinctive whistle.

Cowboys patrolling the herd at night whistled.

Bird watchers practiced their bird calls with whistling.

Fats Waller wrote a song that begins: I love to whistle cause it makes me merry.

That song is entitled truthfully, "I Love to Whistle."

When's the right time to whistle?

Whistle while you work.

Whistling in the dark.

Whistling Dixie.

When you need a big-city cab.

Lauren Bacall famously flirted with future husband and co-actor Humphrey Bogart in the movie *To Have and Have Not* (1944) when she gave him a sideways look and dared him, "You know how to whistle, don't you?" Lauren Bacall asks Humphrey Bogart. "You just put your lips together and blow."

When Bacall left, Bogart gave a slow whistle of appreciation.

Whistling was part of movie musicals and dramas

In the golden age of musicals, productions where music dominated did not arrive fully envisioned.

That categorical designation of musical meant that songs and often dance would dominate the forward motion of what was often a very slender plot. Whistling happened in the background, mostly.

Musicals had predictable plots.

Boy meets girl.
Trouble ensues.
Confusion happens.
Someone intercedes and explains.
Confusion is eased.
Girl understands--and relents.
Boy gets girl.
Music happens—singing and dancing and sometimes, whistling.

Music happens to celebrate the happy ending and other moments

Too, there was a relationship between the old variety shows of Vaudeville which produced a bevy of big-bellowing singers who could sell a song by singing it loudly—so loudly that the people in the back of the auditorium could hear it. Microphones and speakers didn't exist in musical halls of early Vaudeville.

But once that microphone was invented, life on the stage changed. You could hear singers singing.

You could whistle that melody into a microphone, and everyone could hear it too.

Whistling gave singers another way to share a note—to fill space with sound. (It also seemed to put a spring in their step. Whistlers don't plod or slouch.)

Bing Crosby, who started his long and impactful career as one of the Rhythm Boys, broke into whistling intermittently, as he does in the movie *Holiday Inn.*

Whistling is also good for you

Snow White advocates whistling while you work.
In yoga, blowing out air helps you to relax.
In moments of releasing tension, we exhale mightily.
Whistling can do that for you, too. And you don't have to be judged as good or bad at it.

You can simply enjoy Bing Crosby whistling, or you can smile at Lauren Bacall flirting with her future husband.

Watch out! Whistlers tend to become yodelers!

In the "I love to whistle" duet with Bing Crosby, Mary Martin whistles (and yodels). Whether it's her yodeling or her whistling, Bing makes it through their first whistling song, but when Mary Martin goes full-out with the final whistling duet, Bing can't keep up and loses his composure. Yep. When the master whistler tries to join in with Mary, he can't do it. Bing mutters, "I've lost my pucker."

Has that happened to you? Why don't you find out? (Again, you can find that very entertaining duet on YouTube.)

Where is the right place to whistle?

Outdoors. (Some superstitious people believe indoor whistling is unlucky)

If you are a shepherd, when calling your flock. Or your sheep dog.

In Louisburg, NC when they are hosting their annual International Whistling Convention (since 1973).

On a gondola in Venice, if you are the gondolier.

When you are going fishing with Andy and Opie. The opening theme song "The Fishin' Hole" for *The Andy Griffith Show* uses a whistle.

You've got to have a pucker to whistle. So, if it's been a while, since you puckered up, go ahead and pretend you're calling a cab, or Gene Autrey's horse Champion, or the bird sitting outside on a limb. Just put your lips together, honey, and blow.

~

Four YouTube videos are mentioned in this Talk, and the addresses are in the back of the book under the Sources page. They are:

The duet with Mary Martin and Bing Crosby: "I Love to Whistle"

"Que Sera Sera" with Doris Day from the movie *The Man Who Knew Too Much*

The Andy Griffith Show's theme song "The Fishing' Hole"

I Love Lucy Season 4 Palm Springs Episode

SMALL TALK #8

#8 The Andy Griffith Christmas Show

Andy Griffith and Don Knotts

Synopsis
Small Talk #8
The Andy Griffith Christmas Show

Summary: Like many television series, *The Andy Griffith Show* created a Christmas show that has become a classic for viewers and fans. Relying upon the Scrooge motif, Andy represents the Spirit of Christmas Present.

Why I wrote this Small Talk: Like most people who grew up while television also grew up, I love *The Andy Griffith Show,* and was pleased to find the episodes available through Amazon Prime. So, in looking at classic TV series, I re-watched Andy Griffith's Christmas show and was delighted by how the show's writers interpreted the Dickens' character of Scrooge in the cranky Ben Weaver character. I also enjoyed Andy's response and how that affectionate tolerance for Mr. Weaver helped to change him.

Why your group will enjoy this Talk: This episode ends with the Mayberry gang breaking into an easy sing-a-long of a Christmas carol. It's the natural and familiar way that many American homes sang together during the holidays, and it's just sweetly engaging. I think your group will feel like singing together if they re-watch this episode together or are just reminded of it with this Small Talk.

What You Need: It is unlikely that you'll know when this episode will air, but Episode 11 from Season 1 is available to watch on Amazon Prime for free as of the date October 30, 2020.

Tip: Be ready to sing "Away in a Manger" later. And, alert the audience that when you find out that Elinor Donahue has written a "cooking" memoir that includes stories about her time in show business, brace yourself. It's pricey.

Small Talk #8
The Andy Griffith Christmas Show

If when you hear the theme song "The Fishin' Hole" at the beginning of *The Andy Griffith Show,* you feel inclined to whistle along, then you already understand the down-home connection of Mayberry, its citizens, and the stories that have wooed and kept so many viewers for all the time that the show has been re-running.

Maybe you have a favorite Andy Griffith episode.
Maybe it's the one about Aunt Bee's pickles.
Or the one about Otis.
Or Ernest T.
Or Gomer.
Or that time when Barney and Andy…..you fill in the blanks. (And you can ask members of your group to do just that.)

The Andy Griffith Christmas Show happens in Season 1

But the classic Christmas show in the Andy Griffith series happened in Season One. Episode 11 does a take on the old Scrooge motif, with the adversary to Christmas being a local shop keeper named Ben Weaver who finds that one of Mayberry's citizens is making moonshine for his personal pleasure—not to sell. Mr. Weaver objects!

Weaver is a killjoy—a small-town crank who plays the part of Scrooge in this Christmas episode.

The man playing Scrooge is Will Wright, and he looks awfully familiar, doesn't he? And as you watch (re-watch?) this episode, you see Old Ben outside in an alley looking in through a jailhouse window at the Mayberry gang being together in a convivial way.

Mayberry's local Scrooge rejects others before they can reject him

When confronted by the good Christmas spirit of others, Weaver repeatedly barks his own version of "Bah, Humbug!" It's more of an "Aargh!" When Mr. Weaver continues doing it, you don't shake your head and dismiss him; you begin to feel sorry for him—that he doesn't know how to get along with others—to join in the fun. Viewers realize along with Sheriff Taylor that Mr. Weaver rejects others because he feels rejected. Basically, he rejects them before they have a chance to reject him.

Andy represents the spirit of Christmas hospitality

However disagreeable Ben Weaver is, Andy, the Spirit of Christmas Present, keeps forgiving Mr. Weaver and encouraging others in his company to do the same thing.

Intent on trying to clear out the jail cells so that all can enjoy Christmas at home, Sheriff Taylor doesn't want to arrest the accused moonshiner who was just brewing up his elixir for personal use—not commercial, but Mr. Weaver is so insistent they have to lock up their neighbor.

To cushion the blow of separating the man from his family and they from theirs, Andy brings in the moonshiner's family to the jail and invites Barney, Aunt Bee, Opie, and his girlfriend Miss Ellie to have their Christmas party at the jail.

Boisterous and musical fellowship ensues, with Miss Ellie and Andy singing "Away in a Manger." In real life, Elinor was scared to sing with Andy. Her voice shook when she tried. During rehearsal, he coaxed her to practice humming with him at first to ease her nervousness and then got her to sing. It's a lovely rendition.

The sounds of Christmas reach Mr. Weaver the Scrooge, who looks longingly in through the barred window. Once Andy understands that Mr. Weaver is truly outside looking in, he helps Mr. Weaver find a way to join them. And when he comes inside, like Scrooge before him, Mr. Weaver brings gifts with him for others.

A happy Christmas solution to the strain of being separated by ill will and lovelessness occurs. One more Scrooge type finds his heart changed, not by an angel's message or visions revealed by Spirits of Christmas's past or the future, but by what makes Mayberry a place people want to visit, and the citizens who live there are people you wish you could share Christmas with...and sing with, too.

And you can. Because Andy and the Mayberry gang are always with us. And when they sing, we can sing along.

Small Talking Points about the players...

The Players
Will Wright as Ben Weaver
Andy Griffith as Andy Taylor
Don Knotts as Barney Fife
Francis Bavier as Aunt Bee
Elinor Donahue as Miss Ellie
Ron Howard as Opie

William Henry "Will" Wright (Mar 26, 1894-June 19, 1962)

Will Wright as Ben Weaver

Will Wright is so familiar to TV viewers that it may be surprising to learn he made only three appearances on *The Andy*

Griffith Show between 1960-62. We saw Wright elsewhere and just assumed he was always in Mayberry, but he wasn't.

Will Wright routinely played a cranky old man, and you have seen him in all kinds of television series, including *The Real McCoys, The Donna Reed Show, Perry Mason*, and so many others. His last appearance was on an episode of *Bonanza.*

He died in 1962 of cancer in Los Angeles, leaving behind a legacy of performances that are paradoxical: he's the mean old man we all know and love.

Andy Griffith (June 1, 1926-July 3, 2012)

Andy Griffith as Sheriff Andy Taylor

Born in Mount Airy, North Carolina, Andrew Samuel Taylor is as famous for playing Ben Matlock as he is for being likable Sheriff Andy Taylor. Both roles feature the easy-going Griffith as a type of law enforcement officer, which is unexpected if you think about how he began as a gospel singer and as a down-home comedian.

He played a Gomer-esque character in *No Time for Sergeants* (1958)and someone more complex in *A Face in the Crowd* (1957).

So you know Andy Griffith in a variety of ways, but never more lovably than in *The Andy Griffith Show* where everyone, even the lawbreakers, can count on his peace and good will, whether it's Christmas or not.

Griffith was married three times, the first time to Barbara Bray Edwards (1949-1972). His second wife was Solica Cassuto (1973-1981). In 1983, he married his third and last wife Cindy Knight.

After various health struggles, Andy Griffith died of a heart attack in 2012.

Don Knotts (July 21, 1924-February 24, 2006)

Don Knotts as Deputy Barney Fife

After two years on the soap opera *Search for Tomorrow*, Jesse Donald Knotts experienced his first big break on *The Steve Allen Show*. He played a nervous character, and that high-strung quality landed him a role in the Broadway play *No Time for Sergeants*. He reprised that role for the movie by the same name where he met Andy Griffith who took Knotts to Mayberry with him. They were a natural fit—funny, friendly, human.

Knotts won the Emmy five times for his role as Best Supporting Actor in a TV series. Believing the series would end, Knotts began to look for work in movies and left the show in 1965. He moved into roles that capitalized on his nervous persona and starred in *The Ghost and Mr. Chicken* (1966) and made a cameo appearance in *It's a Mad, Mad, Mad, Mad World* (1963).

Knotts continued to appear on television, showing up in a spin-off of *The Andy Griffith Show* when Andy finally married long-time and very patient girlfriend Helen Crump. Knotts also appeared frequently on *The Bill Cosby Show, Here's Lucy,* and *Three's Company.*

When asked what Don Knotts was really like, Betty Lynn, who played Barney's girlfriend on *The Andy Griffith Show,* described Don Knotts as "very quiet. Sweet. Nothing like Barney Fife." That quiet, sweet nature Betty Lynn admired was very attractive to women, and Knotts was something of a ladies' man. He married three times. His first wife was Kathryn Metz (1947-64). His second wife was Loralee Czuchna (1974-1983). His third and last marriage was to Frances Yarborough, from 2002 until his death of respiratory struggles in 2006. Knotts had two children.

∼

Frances Elizabeth Bavier (Dec 14, 1902- Dec 6, 1989)

Frances Bavier plays Aunt Bee

The woman who would become Aunt Bee appeared in the eighth episode of the *Perry Mason show* and then in *Make Room for Daddy,* where she met Andy Griffith. From that meeting, Bavier found her best known role as Aunt Bee to Andy and Opie.

A New York-born woman trained in theatre, Bavier struggled with playing Aunt Bee, believing that the role didn't always ask as much from her as she could give as an actress. People on the set considered her Queen Bee-ish, and later, after the show, she apologized to Andy Griffith on the phone for being difficult at times.

Bavier came to terms with how closely she was identified with the role of Aunt Bee and chose to retire in North Carolina, where she lived a quiet life, having never married. She died of complications from heart disease, breast cancer, and COPD in 1989 and was buried in Siler City.

Mary Elinor Donahue (April 19, 1937—)

Elinor Donahue plays Miss Ellie

Although she started out playing teenage daughter Betty Anderson on *Father Knows Best,* fans of *The Andy Griffith Show* know Elinor Donahue as the gal pharmacist, girlfriend of Andy Taylor, and the kind lady who gave Opie free ice cream. Donahue was under contract for three seasons, but at the end of one season 1960-61, she sought and received a release from her contract with *The Andy Griffith Show*.

Like so many female characters who dated Andy Taylor on the popular show, Donahue left without marrying him and went on to play other parts, most recently a shopkeeper called Bridget who helps Julia Roberts find the right dress to wear in the movie *Pretty Woman* (1990).

In 1998, Donahue published a memoir *In the Kitchen with Elinor Donahue,* which includes some stories about working in

Hollywood and some of her favorite recipes. The mother of four children, she is married to Lou Genevrino (1992).

Ron Howard   (March 1, 1954--)

Andy Griffith and Ron Howard

Who knew that when Ron Howard sang "Oh, oh, the Wells Fargo wagon is a-coming down the street," with Shirley Jones in *The Music Man* (1962), that Ronald William Howard, born in Oklahoma, would not only grow up as one of the most beloved sons in series television but become a crowd-pleasing movie maker as influential and gifted as any cinematic storyteller who has ever lived.

The popular star of another hit series *Happy Days* (1974-80), Howard left television roles to write, direct and produce movies, and his efforts have been crowd pleasing and award winning.

Here's a short list of some of Howard's most popular movies:

Apollo 13 (1995)
How the Grinch Stole Christmas (2000)
A Beautiful Mind (2001) Academy Awards for Best Director and Best Picture
The Da Vinci Code (2006)
In the Heart of the Sea (2015)
Inferno (2016)

Howard married Cheryl Alley in 1975, and the happy couple have four children.

SMALL TALK #9

#9 The Bethlehem Bible Story, Luke Chapter 2

Synopsis
Small Talk #9
The Bethlehem Bible Story

Type: Informative and Interactive

Summary: Sometimes the familiarity of the Bethlehem story causes us to hear it distantly; but when we pay very close attention, we see how it also affirms the divine quest to find the truth and pay homage to it. This Talk presents the Bethlehem story from the Bible and prompts the audience to think about the inherent need we all seem to have to pursue something—a goal, our curiosity, the truth, justice—and the gift of grace, of course. His name is Jesus. He was born in a stable, and the Bible tells the truth about who he is, what his life means to humankind, and why, for many people, Christmas is a holy remembrance.

Why I wrote this Small Talk: Anytime you can get the Bible read out loud you have done your listeners a favor. The Bible has the power to touch people in ways that even music can't. So, I embedded the original Christmas story from Luke chapter 2 into this Small Talk, and while I was re-reading it, I became intrigued by the number of quests in the story.

The Bethlehem story isn't the only one in the Bible that highlights a human's need to follow a quest. You'll find a number of quests described by Jesus in his parables. Remember the lady looking for a lost coin and the man looking for a lost sheep? We are often *found* while searching for something.

Quests keep us going. It doesn't matter how old you are or how mobile. You can have a quest for the truth sitting in your recliner and still enjoy that vitality of asking, knocking, seeking and finding that is possible all the days of your God-given life.

Why your group will savor this Small Talk: There's a good chance no one will be attending a church pageant of the nativity story this year, so this delivery of the original Bible story will be welcome to many. Too, as Charles Dickens says in his *A Christmas Carol,* there can be no experience of Christmas apart from this story that started it all.

Tags: Book of Luke, Mary, Joseph, Simeon, The Wise Men, Anna; **Carols:** Away in a Manger, O Little Town of Bethlehem, Silent Night, O Holy Night, Joy to the World

What you'll need: Someone to read the Bible story from the book of Luke, which is printed here (ESV), or please use your preferred Bible translation. Someone to lead the group in singing Christmas carols, accompanied or not.

Talking Tip: Ask someone other than the speaker to read the Bible story, slowly.

Ice Breaker: Has anyone been to the actual Bethlehem?

Small Talk #9
The Bethlehem Story
Luke Chapter 2

There is another theme of Christmas that is often overlooked in movies of the season. Comedies often try to sneak up on this idea quite superficially in stories about parents seeking the perfect but hard-to-find toy for their child. That's the kind of quest which we view as entertainment. But a real Christmas quest is more important than finding a new-fad gift. A universal Christmas quest in all of us is the drive to find meaning and purpose for our lives.

The quest we all long for from time to time is the one George Bailey discovers in the movie *It's a Wonderful Life* when he realizes his life is not a failure and that he has mattered to others. Scrooge in *A Christmas Carol* learns his lesson the hard way through visits from Spirits – the lesson that we are meant to take care of one another. Both stories are true, but neither story is the complete story of Christmas.

The Christmas stories of George Bailey and Scrooge would have no meaning and purpose if the original Christmas story announcing the birth of Jesus had never happened. It is the story of Jesus that has a ripple effect, causing the lives of others to have meaning and purpose, and that includes George Bailey, Scrooge, and you.

The Bethlehem story is about the universal quest we all share

Perhaps you feel too tired, too old, or you don't have that legendary Christmas spirit that we are supposed to have during this season of evergreen trees and bright lights.

Don't mistake not having a ho-ho-ho spirit for not having the real Christmas spirit, for you do have that, however you feel

For the original Christmas spirit is having a quest for truth and meaning, and having that quest and finding the answers is not contingent upon your energy level, your health, your enthusiasm, or other physical circumstances.

A quest for meaning and purpose rests in the beautiful story of the birth of Christ and what his birth means.

Do you know the answer to that?

While that story of Jesus' birth has been retold in children's church pageants, it's a very grown-up story too and one that becomes yours once you have understood the meaning and purpose that the birth of Christ brings to your life.

Can you say who Jesus is?

One answer is simply this: Jesus is the one who came to fix what Adam broke. And what did Adam break? In the garden of Eden, Adam wanted something not allowed, and in reaching for what was forbidden he broke off an intimate relationship with God. How do you get that relationship back?

Do you want an intimate relationship with God the Father of Lights?

You can have it instantly by simply saying yes to the gift that Jesus brings to the world. He came to fix what Adam broke. Jesus came to make it possible for you to have meaning and purpose in your God-given life by showing up with an invitation to "Come and see" what life inside a faith-created day can become.

That great adventure of living inside the love of God delivered during the original Christmas doesn't begin with the story of Christ's birth. It began in the birth of creation itself, which is found in the book of Genesis. But the redemptive and energizing presence of joy that is possible for everyone— whoever you are-- is announced in the Bethlehem story. Just as the quest of the Wise men to find Christ is celebrated here, their desire to see him ignites in us the quest to know Christ. When we find him, we can know the blessings of loving him.

There are no limitations on who can go looking for Christ.

Finding Christ and following him is not restricted to a time limit or an age limit, and a relationship with him is not about entertainment.

So, you really can't read this story enough, but you can keep reading it.

Read it silently. Then read it aloud. Do you hear it differently?

You will see more and more as you read the story.

But for this time, as you read it, watch how many quests appear in the story. Which people in this story represent being part of a quest? How many fingers do you need to count them, and do you need both hands?

Let's read the Bethlehem story together out loud

Here is chapter 2 from the gospel of Luke (ESV):

SCRIPTURE BEGINS HERE:

2 In those days a decree went out from Caesar Augustus that all the world should be registered. ²This was the first registration when Quirinius was governor of Syria.³And all went to be registered, each to his own town. ⁴And Joseph also went up from Galilee, from the town of Nazareth, to Judea, to the city of David, which is called Bethlehem, because he was of the house and lineage of David, ⁵ to be registered with Mary, his betrothed, who was with child. ⁶ And while they were there, the time came for her to give birth. ⁷ And she gave birth to her firstborn son and wrapped him in swaddling cloths and laid him in a manger, because there was no place for them in the inn.

The Shepherds and the Angels

⁸ And in the same region there were shepherds out in the field, keeping watch over their flock by night. ⁹ And an angel of the Lord appeared to them, and the glory of the Lord shone around them, and they were filled with great fear. ¹⁰ And the angel said to them, "Fear not, for behold, I bring you good news of great joy that will be for all the people. ¹¹ For unto you is born this day in the city of David a Savior, who is Christ the Lord. ¹² And this will be a sign for you: you will find a baby wrapped in swaddling cloths and lying in a manger." ¹³ And suddenly there was with the angel a multitude of the heavenly host praising God and saying,

¹⁴ "Glory to God in the highest,
and on earth peace among those with whom he is pleased!"

¹⁵ When the angels went away from them into heaven, the shepherds said to one another, "Let us go over to Bethlehem and see this thing that has happened, which the Lord has made known to us." ¹⁶ And they went with haste and found Mary and Joseph, and the baby lying in a manger. ¹⁷ And when they saw it, they made known the saying that had been told them concerning this child. ¹⁸ And all who heard it wondered at what the shepherds told them. ¹⁹ But Mary treasured up all these things, pondering them in her heart. ²⁰ And the shepherds returned, glorifying and praising God for all they had heard and seen, as it had been told them.

21 And at the end of eight days, when he was circumcised, he was called Jesus, the name given by the angel before he was conceived in the womb.

Jesus Presented at the Temple

22 And when the time came for their purification according to the Law of Moses, they brought him up to Jerusalem to present him to the Lord **23** (as it is written in the Law of the Lord, "Every male who first opens the womb shall be called holy to the Lord") **24** and to offer a sacrifice according to what is said in the Law of the Lord, "a pair of turtledoves, or two young pigeons." **25** Now there was a man in Jerusalem, whose name was Simeon, and this man was righteous and devout, waiting for the consolation of Israel, and the Holy Spirit was upon him. **26** And it had been revealed to him by the Holy Spirit that he would not see death before he had seen the Lord's Christ. **27** And he came in the Spirit into the temple, and when the parents brought in the child Jesus, to do for him according to the custom of the Law, **28** he took him up in his arms and blessed God and said,

29 "Lord, now you are letting your servant depart in peace,
   according to your word;
30 for my eyes have seen your salvation
31   that you have prepared in the presence of all peoples,
32 a light for revelation to the Gentiles,
   and for glory to your people Israel."

33 And his father and his mother marveled at what was said about him. **34** And Simeon blessed them and said to Mary his mother, "Behold, this child is appointed for the fall and rising of many in Israel, and for a sign that is opposed **35** (and a sword will pierce through your own soul also), so that thoughts from many hearts may be revealed."

36 And there was a prophetess, Anna, the daughter of Phanuel, of the tribe of Asher. She was advanced in years, having lived with her husband seven years from when she was a virgin, ³⁷ and then as a widow until she was eighty-four. She did not depart from the temple, worshiping with fasting and prayer night and day. ³⁸ And coming up at that very hour she began to give thanks to God and to speak of him to all who were waiting for the redemption of Jerusalem.

The Return to Nazareth

³⁹ And when they had performed everything according to the Law of the Lord, they returned into Galilee, to their own town of Nazareth. ⁴⁰ And the child grew and became strong, filled with wisdom. And the favor of God was upon him.

The Boy Jesus in the Temple

⁴¹ Now his parents went to Jerusalem every year at the Feast of the Passover. ⁴² And when he was twelve years old, they went up according to custom. ⁴³ And when the feast was ended, as they were returning, the boy Jesus stayed behind in Jerusalem. His parents did not know it, ⁴⁴ but supposing him to be in the group they went a day's journey, but then they began to search for him among their relatives and acquaintances, ⁴⁵ and when they did not find him, they returned to Jerusalem, searching for him. ⁴⁶ After three days they found him in the temple, sitting among the teachers, listening to them and asking them questions. ⁴⁷ And all who heard him were amazed at his understanding and his answers. ⁴⁸ And when his parents saw him, they were astonished. And his mother said to him, "Son, why have you treated us so? Behold, your father and I have been searching for you in great distress." ⁴⁹ And he said to them, "Why were you looking for me? Did you not know that I must be in my Father's house?" ⁵⁰ And they did not understand the saying that he spoke to them. ⁵¹ And he went

down with them and came to Nazareth and was submissive to them. And his mother treasured up all these things in her heart.

⁵² And Jesus increased in wisdom and in stature and in favor with God and man.

~ The Bible story stops here but the questions continue. ~

You don't need me to name the people who have a quest here, but here they are anyway:

Jesus' parents Mary and Joseph search for a place to rest and have the baby.
Jesus' parents search for Jesus when he goes missing.
What did Simeon want to see?
What did Anna hope to see?
What did the Wise Men in the Bible story hope to see or find?

What are wise men seeking now when they look for Jesus?

By now you have heard some answers in Sunday School, from the pulpit, from friends, from strangers, in books, and on television. You've heard folks who have experienced a born-again rebirth try to explain the transformative event; but until it happens to you, can you know what others are talking about?

Anyone want to offer an answer?

(Pause to give listeners a chance to call out an answer.)

There are many possible ways to answer the question "What are wise men seeking?" One of the responses could be: "I want to live an authentic life."

St. Augustine has another observation:

"Thou hast made us for thyself, O Lord, and our heart is restless until it finds its rest in thee." (St. Augustine *Confessions*)

He also wrote:

"To fall in love with God is the greatest romance; to seek him the greatest adventure; to find him, the greatest human achievement."

You can seek God the Father wherever you are. Right where you are. Right now.

Or you can recall the story of the Prodigal son, who wandered away from his home, found himself broke and eating scraps of food with barnyard animals. That son came to his senses and decided to go home. He made the trip—seeing from afar his father waiting for him in the field. Ready to confess he'd been wrong, the boy kept walking toward the light of his father's love, and even though he knew he was welcome, when he arrived, that boy admitted he had been wrong to leave. That admission-- the declaration that you've wandered away and were wrong-- is called repentance. Say those words to the Father, and you are truly home. Your quest to find home is satisfied, but other quests to know more about God the Father of Lights take its place.

St. Augustine of Hippo was right

Loving God is the great adventure that was made possible by the birth of Jesus in a stable.

You see, read, and hear many stories at Christmas that explore faith and wonder—meaning and purpose. Which story in your life can you tell that explains the quest you have lived out as you look for meaning or as you have defined faith?

Anyone want to share their story?

Does that story change when you tell it to someone? If so, why is that?

To conclude this Talk, ask for carol requests and have your piano player ready for the group to sing the carols that celebrate the Bethlehem story or sing them acapella.

Old favorites include:

Away in a Manger
O Little Town of Bethlehem
O Come All Ye Faithful
Silent Night
O Holy Night
Joy to the World

SMALL TALK #10

#10 Tell Your Pandemic Story in the New Year

Synopsis
Small Talk #10
Tell Your Pandemic Story in the New Year

Type: Informative or Interactive

Summary: We use small stories to tell big truths about how we live our lives. These snapshot stories are often called anecdotes; and while many people believe that an anecdote is always funny, that's not always true. An anecdote is simply the shorthand description or story of an event—happy or sad-- that is told to demonstrate something happened or was learned or is recalled, and the story of that event is told for all kinds of reasons. We all tell our stories. This Small Talk looks at reasons we tell our own stories and what we are trying to say when we do.

Why I wrote this Small Talk: Telling the stories of our lives is natural and the act of telling them is always meaningful. When I read Garson Kanin's description of how Somerset Maugham often repeated the same stories at different dinner tables, I was glad to hear him explain why. Too often, we simply think that repeating stories of our lives means we are developing some kind of memory (or ego) problem. Not true! This Small Talk looks at why we tell our stories and how we are going to tell the next story about how we got through the pandemic in 2020.

Why your group will like this Talk: It may have been a while since anyone mentioned Garson Kanin or Somerset Maugham to your group members, but many of them will know the Tracy and Hepburn movies that Kanin co-wrote with his wife Ruth Gordon (*Adam's Rib* and *Pat & Mike*), and they will most likely remember Maugham's *Of Human Bondage* and *The Razor's Edge*. But do they know why Somerset Maugham repeated himself so often, and can one of his reasons be the same explanation for why we do it? You don't have to be a celebrated writer to have a story worth telling—and to tell it. And tell it again to find the truth of how that past story's event fits into your current understanding of your own life.

What you'll need: A quiet and trusting atmosphere where people can comfortably talk and hear one another. Identify before the Talk occurs a couple of people who will attending and be willing to tell a meaningful story of their lives—maybe a Christmas time story or a New Year's story.

Ice Breaker: Call upon the pre-arranged volunteers to tell their stories.

Small Talk #10
Tell Your Pandemic Story in the New Year

Most likely you have a few signature stories that you have been telling through the years that are your go-to stories.

They represent key moments of learning or change, and sometimes they are referred to as a coming-of-age moment. These stories can be tied to holidays or personal events, joys and calamities.

You have heard many of these stories, and if you have long-time friends, you've heard all of their stories more than once. You know how to listen to them again, and they know how to listen to your stories.

We repeat ourselves all our lives long

As we grow older, we tell the stories again and again or lapse into silence because we can't bear to tell them again.

Writer Garson Kanin (*Adam's Rib; Born Yesterday*), a screenwriter, director and author, calls these frequently told stories "set pieces." In his memoir, *Remembering Mr. Maugham,* Kanin is referring specifically to Somerset Maugham's telling of "set piece" stories at the dinner table with friends, and how through the years Kanin heard the author of *The Razor's Edge* and *Of Human Bondage* tell the same stories seven or eight times the same way using the same words.

As a multi-genre storyteller, Kanin understood why Maugham repeated himself. In settings like ours, we simply wonder if we have run out of small talk or are developing some kind of memory problem.

There are many good reasons to repeat ourselves

But repeating yourself is not a memory problem, really. There are all kinds of valid and completely understandable reasons to repeat yourself in the telling of familiar stories.

One of them is simply to record history.

Another is to try and find meaning in an event even long after it has happened.

Another is to relive the event because it has significance for you, and you want others to understand why or how it was significant. And that understanding actually can change over time. When someone tells the same story again, the teller may be seeing something new, adding the experience to the treasure trove of other experiences along the way, and fleshing out his life's meaning with words.

During Christmas, we tell these "set piece" stories, and like the old movies we watch, they are comforting in their familiarity—feel like home.

We are always gaining and gathering more stories to tell—and which need to be told!

But our go-to set piece stories are not the only stories we have or even the last stories we will tell.

As we live through this lockdown during a pandemic, a season when our moving about has been limited to protect our health, and visitors have been discouraged from coming to visit us to protect theirs (and our health), we find ourselves hearing the news of the day as what's for breakfast, lunch, dinner-- and the report of aches and pains.

It is easy to make the report of aches and pains the news of the day. Sometimes it needs to be because sometimes we need help.

Or understanding.

Or a Tylenol.

But the length, height, and width of our days is not defined by physical space and limitations.

We are still alive with a purpose for being here. Whatever our limitations, we still have a need to live an authentic life, give thanks for wonder which happens in shared kindness and love, and to follow where our faith leads us.

I suspect that you know something you would like to share with someone younger who doesn't know how to avoid certain pitfalls. But by now you have tried to share an experience that if someone could hear it would help that person avoid trouble, heartbreak, and pain. They tune you out.

Do you recall how you still wanted to try and tell them what you know, because we have to try and help others, don't we?

We are trying to be useful, helpful—and in a deep way, redeem the pain of our lives by trying to save someone else from going through that kind of pain.

(Pause for discussion if the group appears to have something to say)

If you want to help, you prove that you have not fulfilled your life's purpose yet. One of our quests is to do the good works appointed for us, and we are always on the lookout for them.

Andy Andrews says there's a reason for why we are still here

Here's what Andy Andrews says in his book *The Noticer* about you and the purpose of your life:

"If you are breathing, you are still alive. If you are alive, then you are still here, physically, on this planet. If you are still here, then you have not completed what you were put on earth to do. If you have not completed what you were put on earth to do … that means your very purpose has not yet been fulfilled. If your purpose has not yet been fulfilled, then the most important part of your life has not yet been lived."
— **Andy Andrews, The Noticer**

Extended periods of isolation and silence can change you. Time to think can refine how you see and think and feel and tell the story of not only this experience of the pandemic but also how you reconsider the significance of your set piece stories you've been telling for a while.

No one's story is over yet

How will you tell this most recent story of the pandemic and the lockdown in the New Year?

Think about your experience of this current pandemic and how you would tell the story of it to others.

And if you have no one to tell your story to immediately, write your story down. Whether you can envision someone reading it or listening to it later, the act of writing down that story has great power. For the act of writing is a quest—like the telling of a story is—to move toward the truth. To seek, find, and name that truth.

You don't have to be a writer to write toward the truth.

And pursuing that truth, even inside a locked down space, is very much worth the effort.

SMALL TALK 11

#11 Auld Acquaintances: A New Year's Talk

Synopsis
Small Talk #11
Auld Acquaintances
A New Year's Talk

Type: Interactive

Summary: This Small Talk opens up a discussion about how we can be a better friend to others and ourselves.

Why I wrote this Small Talk: People find themselves a member of all kinds of groups and often feel different or alone. Those uncomfortable and isolating feelings of being different or alone don't have to discourage us or make us feel like an outcast. Rather, when we recognize them, we can let those feelings remind us that most people feel the same way at one time or another.

I wrote this Small Talk about the auld acquaintances of feeling alone and different to encourage people that they are not as different as they may believe—and when they accept that, they aren't as alone either.

Why your group will enjoy this Small Talk: People sometimes need encouragement to be a better friend to other people and themselves. This Small Talk reminds them that what we perceive as our differences is really a way to recognize all the feelings and fears that we have in common. When we do, we develop the power to love each other better.

What you need: A warm heart, a willingness to change, and what Will Rogers called "a warm curiosity about other people."

When to give this talk: Around New Year's Eve

Ice Breaker Question: Do you remember what Will Rogers said about how he felt about people?

Answer: "I never met a man I didn't like."

Rogers also said, "Even if you're on the right track, you'll get run over if you just sit there."

Small Talk #11
Auld Acquaintances
A New Year's Talk

By the time New Year's Eve arrives, people are often worn out by the disruption to their routine. It is physically and emotionally taxing, and then there's one more social hurdle to jump. You've got to get through New Year's smiling before you can retreat to your interior solitary life in a way that others won't immediately call you a Scrooge, a Loner, or a Crank.

New Year's Eve has its own set of tensions

You can ease many of them by simply setting the clock back three or four hours and toasting the new year in whatever way you prefer at eight o'clock or nine o'clock and then retreating to your room.
Your bed.
Your prayer time.
Your revisiting of what was and envisioning what will come.
And in this way, wherever we are and however we are getting through Christmas and breathing or whistling through New Year's Eve, we share a similar set of auld acquaintances.

We share the experiences of loss and change. These two conditions are everyone's auld acquaintances

While the song we often sing or hum on New Year's "Auld Lang Syne" celebrates the warm memories of people we have known, loved, and miss, the concept of "auld acquaintances" can also refer to the same old experiences that we all share and the same kinds of emotional vacancies and needs we all have and manage the best we can. Pain is a familiar acquaintance these days.

So is loneliness.

Isolation.

Dread.

A lack of energy.

Chronic pain.

Sadness or heartbreak.

Fatigue about facing what's next.

Bracing yourself against spending time with people you don't innately like.

Maybe you are spending time with questions about why people who are your family don't come to see you and what that suggests about the nature of their love and the truth of your relationship which you believed was better than it apparently is.

We love other people who don't always remember us

And here we come to the crux of an issue we all share: we love those who don't necessarily love us to the same depth and commitment we have for them.

We don't stop loving them simply because they don't come to see us for whatever the reason, whether that's the way it was before or the way it has become magnified and true during the lockdown.

So, when you look around or down the hall or next door at people who aren't the people you love best or even like best, you do have something more than your physical location in common with them.

You have the experience of auld acquaintances we all share as human beings: isolation, loneliness, grief, fear, and the surprise of hope which pushes up in you like a sprig of grass rising up through cracks in the concrete or asphalt.

The reality of hope provides us much to celebrate and share. It, too, provides the energy of perseverance to share more of yourself with someone who may not be the person you love best or remember with the greatest longing, but, he or she, like you—is present in the situation where you are.

Could you try to be a better friend to others who live with you?

You can begin to try and be a better friend to your current acquaintances because as a human being growing older you have a great deal in common with the people around you—and they with you, whatever their age, marital status, or how many children they have.

If you live in fear that telling the truth about yourself would result in no one understanding how you feel, find out.

Most likely, many people may feel about their lives the way you feel about yours. That's a surprisingly comforting thing to learn.

The shared knowledge makes people try to be better friends to one another.

An unforgettable and invaluable piece of advice from a preacher who said these words on his knees

Years ago, I heard a minister on his knees beside a new widow. He told her this: "You've got some hard days ahead. Ask God to help you. He will."

I have never forgotten his words.

When you resolve to love others more inside your prayer time, the power of God is present to help you do just that.

He didn't ask us to love one another as ourselves for no reason. What is that reason? To help one another along the way.

And that's another auld acquaintance of human nature

We acknowledge throughout all of our lives moments and times when we have faced something true and made a decision to change. Often, in a refreshed understanding of humility, we admit that need and gratefully accept the real help from God to change, which is what was provided at the original Christmas when Jesus was born.

New Year's Eve is as good a day as any to decide to be a better friend to others and yourself.

Can you say?

"I love you just the way are."

Can you say?

"When I'm gone, don't worry about anything that you might have done or didn't do. I love you just as you were. Are. And all that you will become."

If love feels like the wrong word, try the word "accept." I accept you just as you are.

As you consider acknowledging the love that grows in the fallow field called growing older, know that the people around you are experiencing the same fallow field—know and experience the same hope for a good life for all those that they love and those they are learning to love.

Life is empty and full and plain and beautiful all the days of your life

Appearances that suggest otherwise can be deceiving. At a certain time in our lives we care more about the struggles of the young and how they might grow up with less pain than we do about the current pains we manage.

That's called wisdom, and you have it in a way that Solomon did not.

How can you share it as creatively and effectively as Charles Dickens did with his story about Scrooge or even a haphazard angel called Clarence did in the movie about an ordinary guy called *It's a Wonderful Life?*

That can be one of the mysteries you try to solve when you wake up tomorrow.

That can be your quest, and we never stop having something to do like looking for an answer only we alone can find out.

We are all still here together. What can we do more than love one another?

Enjoy the quest of living a life warmed by love for others—and they for you. Charles Dickens through Jacob Marley and Scrooge warned cold-hearted people about the consequences of being self-absorbed. Frank Capra through the story of George Bailey assured you that every life matters, and every life touches many other lives.

You can afford to love others because there's plenty of love to go around. Nothing—not age or separation of others—can separate you from the love of God and as a blessing of that love, freely give it away as often as you can.

Happy New Year.

Sources & YouTube Addresses

Andrews, Andy, *The Noticer*
Barrett, Mary Ellin Berlin, *Irving Berlin, a Daughter's Memoir*
Capra, Frank, **The Name Above the Title, An Autobiography**
Clooney, Rosemary, **Girl Singer: A Memoir of the Girl Next Door**
Crosby, Bing, **Call Me Lucky**
Dickens, Charles, **A Christmas Carol**
Giddins, Gary, **Bing Crosby: Swinging on a Star the War Years**
Giddins, Gary, **Bing Crosby: A Pocketful of Dreams, The Early Years**
Gottfried, Martin, **Nobody's Fool The Lives of Danny Kaye**
Handy, W. C., **Father of the Blues**
Kanin, Garson **Remembering Mr. Maugham**
Munn, Michael Munn, **Jimmy Stewart: The Truth Behind the Legend**
O'Hara, Maureen, **'Tis Herself**
St. Augustine of Hippo, **Confessions**
Wagner, Robert, **Pieces of My Heart**

YouTube addresses for clips referenced:

Small Talk #3

"What'll I Do?" Sung by Rosemary Clooney
https://www.youtube.com/watch?v=Ffcy3jg14yc
   Time: 3 minutes and 4 seconds

"God Bless America" sung by Irving Berlin
https://www.youtube.com/watch?v=Vmc-pEyUHTs
   Time: 2 minutes and 7 seconds

"Oh, How I Hate to Get Up in the Morning, " sung by Irving Berlin https://www.youtube.com/watch?v=7OFVFxXpY_8
Time: 2 minutes and 4 seconds

Small Talk #4
Fred Astaire Cuts Loose at the Oscars 1970
https://www.youtube.com/watch?v=CnrbdNjf-aw&t=148s
   Time: 7 minutes and 33 seconds

"The Waiter and the Porter and the Upstairs Maid" sung by Bing Crosby and Mary Martin
https://www.youtube.com/watch?v=_0e1DF4TUYY
Time: 3 minutes and 37 seconds

Small Talk #7
 Doris Day singing Que Sera Sera from The Man Who Knew—
https://www.youtube.com/watch?v=ja0sYgAiak8
Four minutes and five seconds

You know how to whistle don't you? Lauren Bacall and Humphrey Bogart
https://www.youtube.com/watch?v=i9Ay727EYzw
3 minutes and 16 seconds

The Andy Griffith Theme Song:
https://www.youtube.com/watch?v=S_xFuWmdhLk
two minutes

I Love to Whistle Duet: Mary Martin and Bing Crosby
https://www.youtube.com/watch?v=TtxOaMnoUbg
Time: 6 minutes and 35 seconds

I Love Lucy Rock Hudson Whistling episode
Season 4 Palm Springs episode
https://www.youtube.com/watch?v=UjLlcSBH0bQ
3 minutes and half

Small Talk #8
Andy Griffith's Christmas Show "Away in a Manger"
https://www.youtube.com/watch?v=ZVD6uSydxdU
One minute and forty-eight seconds

Bonus Excerpt: Mildred Budge in Cloverdale

Visit from a Cereal Killer

Retired school teacher Mildred Budge was standing naked in her laundry room remembering how her friend Cleo had died in the same state of undress, when she heard her front doorbell ring the first time. It couldn't be anyone she knew. All of Mildred Budge's friends knew to use the back door by the kitchen.

The timing was bad.

Mildred thought maybe she would just let whoever had come to the wrong house go away, when the doorbell rang again. And then, again. Insistently.

There was no ignoring it.

Only Mildred was naked, and everything she had been wearing while tagging dusty, mite-ridden furniture in the hot attic was now rotating inside the washing machine. On top of the clothes dryer were three lone unmatched black socks and one set of long underwear: white cotton Cuddl Duds that Mildred had intended to put away until the following winter.

As the bell rang five more times, Miss Budge decided that any clothes were better than none. Damp with perspiration and gritty with dust, she grabbed the Cuddl Duds and began the arduous task of wriggling into them. It wasn't easy. She looked down at herself in the clingy wintertime underwear that fit like a diaphanous white body stocking.

Victoria's Secret would not be hiring her pear-shaped frame to model lingerie.

"Miz Bulge! Are you all right in there?" A man's voice called out.

Her morning caller knew her, but she didn't recognize his voice. She heard the front doorknob jiggled impatiently. With a start, Miss Budge couldn't remember if she had locked the front door after bringing in the morning newspaper.

"I'm on my way!" Miss Budge called out, and her voice broke. Living alone with no one to talk to for long periods of time, one's voice became, occasionally, untrustworthy.

Tugging at the snug shirt that wanted to rise up and show her unpierced navel, Miss Budge hastily detoured to the foyer, pausing on the other side of her own front door to check the lock.

She peered through the peephole.

Miss Budge had never formally met her morning caller, but she did recognize him. Standing on her front door step was the young father who had moved with his wife and son into the old Garvin house across the street. The young man was wearing the same clothes she had always seen him in--faded black jeans and a black T-shirt. However, this was the first time the young father was close enough for Miss Budge to read the words stenciled on the front of the T-shirt: "Cereal Killer."

He was holding a large Ziploc bag with lumpy grains in it.

As she sent a news flash prayer to Jesus—'There's a cereal killer at my front door and I'm not fully dressed'—she called out, "Another moment, dear boy! I'll be right with you."

Miss Budge scooted to her bedroom and hurriedly slipped into her thick white chenille robe that she had bought for $19 at an after-Christmas sale three months ago. Adrenaline pumping, she clumsily pushed her still naked feet into sage green plastic Crocs. They were the ugliest shoes she had ever seen, but astonishingly comfortable.

"Miz Bulge! Is everything okay in there?" The Cereal Killer pounded on the door this time. Three hard raps.

Miss Budge cinched the thick robe firmly around her waist and scurried back to the front door, the toe of her right Crocs catching on the rug. She stumbled, and her arms batted the air as she fought to keep her footing. She got her balance back as the doorknob rattled again noisily.

"You haven't fallen or something, have you?" he called through the door.

Miss Budge wrenched the cold brassy doorknob and swung the front door open.

"Of course, I have not fallen. Why would I?" Even as Miss Budge said the words, she remembered so many of her older friends for whom the end of their mobility was signaled by a commiserating tsk-tsk-tsk from every messenger who had ever delivered the dreaded news, "Oh, did you hear? She fell."

Cleo had fallen down naked in her laundry room and died alone. And she wasn't the only one of Mildred's acquaintances to begin that journey toward dependence on others in a hospital, nursing home, or assisted living with a fall.

Blinking at the mid-morning sunlight, Miss Budge offered a disciplined, cordial smile, one that had developed over twenty-five years of greeting scared fifth graders as a public-school teacher and which had not diminished in the past two years since her retirement. "Young man, what is it you require so urgently?"

"Miz Bulge?" The Cereal Killer confirmed, squinting downward to meet her brown-eyed gaze. "You're shorter than they said."

"Why would people discuss my height?" Miss Budge inquired immediately, meeting his gaze unwaveringly, though she had to look up to do so. Her neighbor was tall and lanky with the kind of loose posture and untoned muscles that indicates a dearth of exercise.

"No. They said you was a great teacher, and somehow I jess thought you would be taller," he finished lamely. "I'm Kenny from across the street," he announced with a tip of his head toward the old Garvin house. "We been meaning to come say hi. The wife sent this to you," Kenny declared, holding out a gallon-size plastic Ziploc bag of what appeared to be rolled oats with raisins and slivered almonds.

Miss Budge reached politely for the proffered bag. Gifts of food usually came in covered white paper plates or disposable tin pans that she and her friends from the Berean Sunday school class chose to use when taking food to someone's house.

Miss Budge held the cellophane bag of grains up to the foyer light as if it were a bottle of special wine whose color she wanted to check. "How thoughtful," she murmured. "Won't you come in, Kenneth?"

"Thank you, Miz Bulge," Kenny said, stepping into her foyer. A heavy silver key chain slapped against his leg. He patted it companionably as if it were a small pet that was keeping him company. Squared bluish-black marks that reminded Miss Budge of some ancient Celtic designs set off his otherwise unmarred youthful hands.

When she peered more closely Miss Budge saw that the cribbed symbols were not a mysterious message in need of decoding but a single letter tattooed on each knuckle across the back of his hand that ultimately spelled out: L-O-V-E. Although she did not understand the allure of what amounted to inking graffiti upon one's person, Miss Budge, a spinster Christian lady, did believe in love. She smiled beneficently, as she adjusted the beige rheostat light switch in her expansive foyer.

The overhead light grew brighter, illuminating the various black and white photos on the wall of southern bridges that she had collected at one time in her life. Miss Budge had once upon a time loved the sight of aged bridges—loved the lines and arcs and the hope of them, shores being connected so people could cross over. But that season in her life had passed. The pictures were still hung, now a memorial to her previous affection for them rather than a celebration of the old-timey bridges themselves.

Kenny blinked rapidly, confused. She saw that Kenneth's eyes were a weak blue. Underneath the baseball cap that he did not take off, she assumed he was losing his hair prematurely.

"My last name is Budge. You have been calling me Miz Bulge," the retired teacher explained. She patted her midsection. She was plumper than she had ever been. A frequent awareness of her increasing pear shape had not stopped the pounds from accruing, however. "But it's Mildred—Mildred Budge. Miss…." she declared forthrightly, unashamed of her singleness.

Kenny espied the pictures of solitary bridges on the walls. He blinked some more. The wispy, brown goatee on his chin waved gently when he spoke.

"Miz Deerborn told me about you."

"Will you sit down?" Miss Budge said, waving toward her living room. Her hands were bare of rings. She didn't wear jewelry when she had work to do, and she had spent a sticky morning in her hot attic tagging stored furniture that was to be taken and delivered to The Emporium, a local antique warehouse and flea market. She and her best friend Fran Applewhite were opening a sales booth.

Their initial inventory was the content of their respective attics: two lifetimes of acquired antiques (and a fair amount of old furniture) that would make them a fortune, predicted Fran--or at least enough money so they could travel some.

"I won't stay long," Kenny promised, stepping carefully as if he didn't want to leave footprints on the glossy wooden floor. Kenneth's navy and white athletic shoes made the same small sticking sound against the taffy-colored hardwood floor as her green Crocs. As if mesmerized, her visitor revolved slowly, taking in the room before sitting down on the yellow chintz sofa and saying with wonder, "It's so clean in here."

Miss Budge automatically surveyed her living room, pausing to twist the clear plastic prismatic rod that opened her front mini-blinds. The room filled with sunlight. As the room grew brighter, Miss Budge saw that she needed to dust again. There was a small scrap of clipped white paper which must have escaped her paper shredder resting on the border of the large red and blue oriental carpet that defined the floor space. In a culture that necessarily lived with the threat of identity theft, Miss Budge had become a dedicated shredder of her monthly bills on which the numbers, if obtained, could facilitate the stealing of her credit cards, bank accounts, and most importantly, her identity. While shredding was yet another routine chore, Miss Budge liked doing it. She had invested in a sturdy stand-alone monster shredder from Costco that was stationed next to the telephone table, a superior style of furniture made sadly obsolete by cell phones.

Itching to pick up that errant scrap of white paper that disturbed her sense of order, Miss Budge said instead, "Kenneth, are you thirsty?" She had not lost that school teacherly tone. "Do you want a drink?" Her head bobbed up and down encouragingly. When she did, her brown curls caught the light, creating a halo effect that she would have enjoyed if she had known it was happening. She didn't.

"It's too early for me," Kenny said, sitting back on the sofa. "But you go ahead and take a drink if you need a little something. I know how it is. I've got a granny who likes her wine in the morning, too."

Miss Budge's spine lengthened as her posture aligned itself with the truth.

"I do not need something to drink," she said, taken aback. Her forehead furrowed, deepening the lines that had grown from squinting while grading endless stacks of compositions written by students who did not have good penmanship. Miss

Budge absent-mindedly massaged the tender place between her eyebrows that felt now like it retained some perpetual nerve damage. Then, she pressed her brown plastic eye glasses up on her nose; they slipped periodically. Soon, it would be time to go see Mr. Cates. He had been keeping her glasses adjusted for thirty years.

"Me and my wife moved in to that old house two months ago," Kenny said, with a jut of his whiskery chin toward the old Garvin house across the street.

Since Ron Garvin had died of some kind of dementia the legality of his last will had been questioned, and the potential heirs were fighting over his estate. The Garvin house was being rented out by the executor until the domicile could be legally sold and the profits distributed.

"Linda didn't want to live in Old Geezerville," Kenny explained, apparently unaware that the castigation of the Garden District in Montgomery, Alabama as Old Geezerville might be insulting to someone who had lived there her whole life.

The old geezers in reference were the long-time citizens of a southern city that had not only been the birthplace of the civil rights movement, but was also the home place of Zelda Fitzgerald, a famous belle and the wife of F. Scott. For those who cared, country singer Hank Williams was buried over at Oakwood Cemetery not too far from where Nathaniel Coles had lived when he was four years old with his family. In his teens he dropped the "s" and became Nat King Cole.

"I finally talked Baby into it. Our house is awesome. Really awesome, you know. We have what they call an attic fan. You can turn it on and open the windows. The air comes through just like the air conditioner was on," Kenny bragged. "It's going to save us a ton of money this summer, and it's already getting hotter by the day. We believe in going green." Kenny stared out at his own home through Miss Budge's front window and took a deep breath.

"Me and the wife make organic cereal. That's what I brought you right there. It'll get you going regular. That's our sales hook. These days, you either sell to people who can't sleep, can't lose weight, or to people who can't...." Kenny struggled for the word he needed, pressing his thin lips together, and finally settled on, "Who can't *go*. Cereal can't help you sleep," Kenny added lamely. "Although if that's all you ate, you probably could lose some weight."

There was an awkward pause.

Miss Budge could not discern Kenny's real purpose in coming to see her. Had he caught a glimpse of her and decided she needed to go on a diet?

Miss Budge was an unabashed size-14 woman, but fleshing out the seams of one's garments seemed to happen inevitably as one grew older. The better part of wisdom was to practice moderation in eating, walk as much as you could, and then accept your anatomy as it developed.

Miss Budge eyed the Cereal Killer with curiosity. It seemed unlikely to her that any newcomer would make it his personal mission to infiltrate an older neighborhood and then call on the plumper residents with the goal of putting them on a cereal diet in order to sell his product. Still, she could not recall a time in her life when anyone other than the doctor had ever brought up the subject of her regularity. She decided that the prudent course would be to change the subject.

"I know you are new to the neighborhood. It is actually referred to as Cloverdale—to some, Old Cloverdale," the retired school teacher explained patiently. When Kenny blinked as if he didn't speak English, she explained, "Cloverdale is considered to be the heart of historic Montgomery."

Kenny blinked some more, as if he didn't recognize the name of the city where they lived. Miss Budge smiled encouragingly, and continued politely. "I wonder if you have visited the Fitzgerald museum yet? It is to your left, about two miles that way," Miss Budge directed, pointing, and one more time, saw her mother's hand. She did not mind the vision of her mother's hand extending from her arm at all. Though no one expected a woman of Miss Budge's age to miss a parent, Mildred Budge still did miss her mother and was glad for the company of even the image of her mother's hand.

Kenny eyed the older woman as if she were speaking a foreign language. His eyes morphed to a weak shade of green. Miss Budge wondered if Kenneth was weak or just young. She had taught many young people and had learned that looking into their eyes and making assessments about intelligence or character based on an expression or shade of eye color had very little to do with who they really were—no more than how people once used to feel the bumps on a person's cranium to determine intelligence. Knowing that (and it had taken her a surprisingly long time to learn it) Miss Budge often fought the impulse anyway to know person's head shape with her fingertips, like a blind person might. Kenny had a rectangular-shaped head. Her fingers began to strum the air gently. If she could know the contours of his head with her hands, what would the arcs and bumps tell her about what was going on inside? She clasped her hands determinedly in her lap and held them there while surreptitiously checking the closure of her robe.

Her mother would have liked this robe, too, she thought—and smiled.

"The museum is the old house of a famous Montgomery family. F. Scott Fitzgerald is a famous author. He married a Montgomery girl," she explained patiently. "You may recall from your high school days that Fitzgerald wrote *The Great Gatsby*."

Kenny stared at Miss Budge blankly, and the color of his eyes deepened to the color of an ocean just before it rained. Troubled, Kenny tried to figure out what to say next.

When he didn't immediately speak, Miss Budge continued. "His wife Zelda Sayre was not only a famous southern belle here but a talented writer as well."

Kenny's fingertips scratched the tops of his thighs as if he were getting ready to explain the purpose of his visit. Miss Budge nodded encouragingly, but Kenny did not respond to her cue.

"Or, there's Martin Luther King, Jr.'s church downtown or The First White House of the Confederacy," she added, sounding like one of those volunteer tour guides that some senior citizens become to fill their days after they retired. Though she was retired—prematurely, according to some—she was still too busy to volunteer in that capacity.

Kenny blinked and said, "Awesome." He rubbed his palms on the tops of his jeans. The silver chain with the keys jangled. He petted it.

Miss Budge felt impatient then, though she hid it. Fran and Winston were coming over with the truck in a half hour, and she needed to shower and dress before they arrived. Certainly, the delivery of cereal could not have been Kenneth's primary goal. "Are you sure you don't want some lemonade?" his hostess prompted. She could get it, he could drink it, he could leave.

Kenny shook his head, no, looking as if he might rise. But he didn't. "Miz Bulge...."

Determined to be polite, Miss Budge sat back in the uncomfortable turquoise chair. She had forgotten how unforgiving the chair was. Miss Budge shifted her derriere, struggling for a different center of gravity that might ease the rigidity, but she did not find it.

"Miz Bulge," Kenny said, beginning again, his gaze drifting around the room. "I been watching your house, and you go to church on Sundays. You carry a Bible and everything," Kenny declared. And his nervous hands came to a rest on the tops of his thighs, as he looked to his right at the table with the reading lamp. There were three different Bibles on it.

Kenny's eyes caught hers, and he pressed on. "My son is not a friendly boy. It's like he's not even there sometimes, you know? He's seven. He's supposed to be in school; but Baby---Linda, my wife---thinks Chase won't fit in at school because of his not talking. She's been trying to home school him, but it ain't going as well as she hoped it would. Baby's not a teacher, don't you see?" Kenny said, and his tattooed fingers began to strum the tops of his black-denimed thighs again, spelling out L-O-V-E over and over again.

Miss Budge nodded almost imperceptibly, and the warmth in her brown eyes faded to a wary watchfulness.

"You being a schoolteacher and all…"

Mildred assumed the 'and all' referred to going to church on Sunday and carrying a Bible.

"And I hear you still go to houses of sick kids sometimes…."

"Not anymore," Mildred replied carefully. Initially, after her sudden decision to retire two years ago--and because she needed the money to supplement her reduced fixed income--Miss Budge had accepted short-term assignments as a teacher for homebound students.

But she hadn't done that work for long. The children were too sick and too brave, and they had asked Miss Budge questions that were too hard to answer. She knew the answers; she just didn't want to say them out loud to young children in pain.

Kenny slapped the tops of his black jeans and finally got to his point. "I was wondering if you could help my boy."

"I am not a doctor," Mildred Budge replied, postponing the polite but firm 'no' she would offer Kenny in a moment just as soon as she framed it in her mind. She had left that kind of work behind--cried as many tears as she could. Besides, it was never wise to get caught up in the neighbors' domestic problems, especially if they lived as close as across the street. Before she could say no, her telephone rang.

Loudly.

Miss Budge had only one phone, and she kept the ringer on 'Loud' so that she could hear it ring anywhere in the house. She always answered her phone calls beside her wooden telephone table where a writing tablet and pen were readily available for note-taking and where the small seat built into the table gave her a place to rest in case the caller was long-winded. She sat there to do her monthly shredding, too. Other people thought that speaking on the telephone or shredding the monthly bills were tasks that happened in concert with other activities; it was called multitasking. But Mildred Budge did not like splitting her attention; she liked being focused, had learned as a school teacher that giving one's attention to a person or a job resulted in a better understanding of that person and a better job when work was to be done.

Kenny waited for Miss Budge to move and answer the telephone. She did not.

"I don't answer the telephone when I have a guest," Miss Budge explained simply as the ringing continued, then stopped abruptly.

Kenny laughed. Genuinely. As if the explanation of good manners was some kind of joke. "Miz Deerborn said you was funny and for me not to be afraid of you."

Ah, Belle Deerborn. The well-intentioned woman—and a good friend, too-- who lived just behind Mildred Budge on the other side of the circle that connected their intersecting yards.

Kenneth leaned forward and said in what was almost a whisper: "Miz Belle said you have the gift of healing kids."

Immediately, Miss Budge began to shake her head, no. "I was a teacher. That is all," she replied firmly. "You are wrong—and so is Belle—if you think otherwise."

"Miz Deerborn said you would say that," Kenny replied immediately, his brown wispy goatee wagging.

"It is the truth," Miss Budge replied unswervingly. "I do not glamorize the fruits of determined work by calling it something it is not."

11 Holiday DIY Small Talks

Kenneth nodded as if he were in on the conspiracy of discretion that Miss Budge was determined to perpetuate. "Maybe you could jess speak to my boy then," he said with a wink. "Jest your speaking to him would be good, 'cause Chase don't talk to nobody, even us, sometimes." Kenny took an anxious breath and switched tactics, attempting to persuade her. "That cereal I brought you is all organic. 'S very good for you. No chemicals, pesticides, etcetera, etcetera, etcetera. Let me know if you like it, and I'll bring you a bunch more." Kenny stood up then suddenly. He had finished the job he had given himself to do. The sun shifted from behind a cloud and spilled fresh illumination into the room right where he was standing. The angles of his square-shaped head were easily discerned as bumps inside the baseball cap he had never removed. Miss Budge read his mind then: he had come to see the lady across the street, brought her his offering, made his request, and now he was going home.

Miss Budge was ready for him to go, and she stood more slowly, not because she was older or creaky or less able to stand, but because in her generation one did not rush others out the door by rising too quickly. There was always a hint in every gesture that parting was sweet sorrow—really.

Miss Budge smiled as she followed him to the foyer, speaking in the pace of having an infinite amount of time to get to know other people that others erroneously and inappropriately judged harshly as an irritating habit of an older person, but it was only courtesy. "That explains why the UPS truck comes to your house so often. He must be bringing you supplies for your organic cereals," she theorized aloud, as Kenny led the way to her front door.

Kenny's voice grew proud. "We sell on the internet a lot, and we take it over to the health food store on the Easter by-pass. We have mucho customers now," Kenny said proudly, as her telephone began to ring again. "Somebody really wants to talk to you," Kenny said. "I'll go on and get out of your way."

He turned in the doorway and said, his voice growing quieter: "My boy's name is Chase, and you don't know him yet, but he's special."

Miss Budge met the young father's gaze, so similar to the faces of so many young parents of young children who had been in her care during the twenty-five years she had served the state in the public-school system. Kenny was a stranger, but Miss Budge knew him. Kenny was a young father who had a son who was special.

"You could come over any time. Any time at all that suits you. Linda would love to meet you," Kenny promised, looking across the street to his new home where the blinds were closed, and no lights appeared to be on inside. There was something in that anxious glance at his own home that moved Miss Budge. She relented.

"I'd be delighted to meet your Chase," Mildred agreed, casting an involuntary glance at the insistent telephone as it continued to ring.

Kenneth fired an imaginary pistol at her with his forefinger and thumb, and Miss Budge marveled at a hand gesture that spoke of a violence that was inconsonant with the nature of his request. Still, she fought the urge born of politeness to mimic Kenneth's hand movement, offering a short wave of farewell instead as she walked toward the telephone. On the way, Mildred stooped over and picked up the scrap of white paper that had been bothering her. It was a piece of notebook paper, not a piece of a shredded bill.

"Greetings to you and yours," Miss Budge said, answering the phone.

"Have you been drinking?" Fran Applewhite asked sharply.

Before Mildred could answer, Fran said, "That was me calling before; but then I thought you might be in the attic, and if I let it keep ringing, you might break your neck trying to answer the telephone. You don't want to die in the attic. It would have been hard as all get-out to bring your body down those stairs.

Remember how hard it was to get the broken water heater down? So, I hung up and waited a spell. I have news. It's big," Fran warned.

"I was not in the attic. I was in my living room talking with a cereal killer who thinks that the Eastern by-pass is named after Easter Sunday or the Easter bunny. It is unclear which one he has in mind."

Fran interrupted her. "Mildred, she's killed another one."

Mildred didn't have to ask who Fran meant. She knew. Liz Luckie had recently married for the fourth time; and each time, the husbands had died early in the marriage. Mildred had not known the first three husbands, but she had been a special friend of Liz's most recent groom.

"How did Hugh die?" Mildred asked. She sat down heavily in the small seat built into the telephone table. It was a tight fit. It didn't use to be.

"The regular way. Natural causes." Fran reported bluntly.

"Natural causes. Again," Mildred repeated bleakly. She patted her face with one hand. She felt pale. Then, she pressed the same hand to her chest. Her heart was beating fast. The chenille robe was thick. She was wearing long underwear, too, but Mildred felt chilled. Her lower lip trembled. No hot flash conveniently arrived when it might have helped to warm her.

"They all die of natural causes," Fran said quietly. She hesitated before adding, "Today's Thursday. I figure the funeral will be Saturday."

Mildred nodded into the telephone, her throat instantly dry. Yes. That might be hard for someone else to arrange, but for a woman who had already orchestrated three funerals for her previous husbands, arranging a funeral in two days would not be a problem. She wouldn't have the funeral on a Sunday afternoon, and Monday was too late.

"I wanted to tell you before Winston and I got there together with his truck because that's not the kind of news you need to hear in front of company," Fran explained, her voice dropping to a whisper.

Winston must have come inside Fran's house and was now standing near enough to Fran to hear what she was trying to tell Mildred quietly.

Mildred swallowed hard, remembering how before Hugh had married Liz, his fingertips had grazed hers in the church kitchen when he had handed her his water glass to be washed on a Saturday morning. Each had volunteered to participate in the deep spring cleaning of the church building.

And before that, Hugh had sat beside her in Sunday school as if he just happened to land there and how nervous his sitting close had made her feel—and crowded.

And Hugh had asked her to dance after one of the church weddings at the country club, and she hadn't said no fast enough. Hugh had taken her in his arms and steered her around, and while they moved—scuttled crablike is how Mildred described it to herself—about the floor, she had endured an embarrassing hot flash and broken out in a flop sweat of sorts that Hugh didn't seem to notice, but, of course, he had noticed.

"I've got to go now, Millie. It'll be all right," Fran whispered before hanging up. Mildred's best friend said the words with the authority of a veteran widow who had told herself the same thing through many a long night spent without Gritz who had died on her—the husband Fran Applewhite had loved dearly for forty-three years

Books by Daphne Simpkins

Lovejoy, a novel about desire
Miss Budge Goes to Fountain City, a Christmas story
The Mission of Mildred Budge, a collection of fictional and often funny short stories about missions in the life of a church
Miss Budge in Love, fictional short stories about church life in the South
Mildred Budge in Cloverdale, the first full-length novel about Southern church lady Mildred Budge
Mildred Budge in Embankment, the sequel to Cloverdale
Christmas in Fountain City, a Southern Christmas small-town story
Blessed, essays about caregiving
What Makes a Man a Hero? A collection of essays about men for Father's Day
What Al Left Behind, essays about the positive benefits of caring for a dementia patient
A Cookbook for Katie, a memoir masquerading as a cookbook written for a niece about to get married

The Long Good Night, a memoir about caregiving for an Alzheimer's patient

***Nat King Cole:* An Unforgettable Life of Music,** a biography for children about Nat King Cole

About the author
Daphne Simpkins

Daphne Simpkins is a lifelong unabashed eavesdropper on other people's conversations and lives, which has resulted in her writing books and essays about church life in the South, cooking, and caregiving. Along the way, she earned a spot on the speakers' bureau for the Alabama Humanities Foundation and has been going around the state giving longer talks than the ones in this Small Talk book about all kinds of subjects, including Will Rogers, Nat King Cole, Olympia Brown, Betty Crocker and Aunt Jemima, and the American Songbook. She didn't want to stop talking about them either, but the lockdown muzzled her, too, and since she can't leave the house, she converted some of her Talks to these user-friendly versions that she hopes leaders of Zoom groups and Assisted Living Directors will find helpful. You can let her know if they do by finding her on Facebook, Twitter, Linkedin.com and BookBub.

Manufactured by Amazon.ca
Bolton, ON